LOVE
IS
THE
ONLY
TRUTH

To Sharmini

With Love
Gill and Dear Don
xx

LOVE
IS
THE
ONLY
TRUTH

DENNY DAKIN

CO AUTHOR GILL WILKINSON
FOREWORD DR. CLINT G. ROGERS

LOVE IS THE ONLY TRUTH
by Denny Dakin
co author Gill Wilkinson

Published by Wisdom of the World Press
www.MyAncientSecrets.com

ISBN-13: 978-1-952353-95-6
eISBN: 978-1-952353-94-9

Cover design: Jason Wilkinson
Interior design: Maggie McLaughlin

Printed in the United States

Contents

Gill, Donna Eden & Denny

Praise for
Love is the only truth

It is an honour for me to endorse Denny Dakin's book, and it was a privilege to have known her. For this woman to have turned out so glorious and simply a spirit of love, it is meaningful to understand how far she came. Her life began in an orphanage where she was severely and constantly abused.

It is very special to read about her journey from finding herself through her love of music; the study of mathematics with her stepfather, who helped her to trust; and psychotherapy; but mostly, through following her guides.

All her life, Denny had spirit guides who helped her to love herself and love everyone, even those who had harmed her. Love became everything for Denny, and she leaves wisdom about her journey in this lovely book. You will find it so very easy to read and enjoy.

Donna Eden
Author of *Energy Medicine*
2023

Foreword

As I boarded the plane to England to attend her funeral, my eyes clouded with tears.

I reflected on how Denny Dakin is one of the most remarkable people I've ever had the honour of knowing.

At age 80, Denny could easily be described as irreverent (a rule-breaker), extraordinary, outrageous, stubborn, witty, kind, and gloriously loving. To me, she was like a combination of Mother Teresa & Nelson Mandela – she'd experienced the most horrific things in her life, intense pain, abuse & abandonment, and found a way to transmute all of that with forgiveness and pure love.

Because she had done this for herself, I witnessed her support many other people from around the world to also do this, including myself. She would open us to our hidden wounds and help us find healing with the power of truly learning to love in new and 'unreasonable' ways. Unreasonable – because love is beyond reason.

Shortly after meeting her, I felt a strong impression that her life story should be shared with the world. My sense was that if more people knew about her transformational healing process, it could have the effect of helping heal their hearts, too.

Now sitting on the plane headed to her funeral, I am looking out the window at the ocean. I smiled thinking of the first time I met Denny. Her daughter Clare had requested I help Denny with some pressing health challenges, using some of the ancient healing methods I'd been trained in. Denny's enthusiasm when it worked was priceless.

Then, along with hundreds of people from over 30 countries, Denny and her dear friend Gill (who you'll also 'meet' and fall in love with through this book) ended up joining a course I was leading, called the 100-Days Ancient Secrets Experience.

Denny spoke on several of the global calls, mentioning the opening quote in the book *Ancient Secrets of a Master Healer*, which says:

> "I didn't come to teach you.
> I came to love you.
> Love will teach you."

Denny shared such practical ways in which she had made love her teacher, and inspired us all so much that an entire team of volunteers from around the world began working to capture her wit and wisdom, in order to create this book that you now hold.

The 100-Day course completed, and months later everything had been captured that was needed for this book.

Shortly after that is when Denny completed her life's journey and her Spirit left her body.

As the plane approached England, I looked in my bag and saw the graduation certificate from the 100-Day course that I hadn't had the chance to give Denny while she was alive.

Although any passing of a loved one can bring up a lot of emotions, as I landed in England I felt a sweet, peaceful joy for many reasons:

- I felt grateful to have met Denny, and know how fully she lived her life;

- I was touched to think of all the laughter, all the love, and all the healing she brought to this planet... even after experiencing such horrific experiences as a child;
- And I was humbled that we had fulfilled one of her greatest desires, to put these things into a book, so that her soul could leave her body in peace. I was touched how many of the other participants in the 100-Day course showed up for the funeral service or watched it online.

Before we arrived, we were told this was a 'celebration of life', and we were invited to dress in colorful clothes.

The service for Denny started by Liz saying, "we are not here to say goodbye, as there is no such a thing – you are always with us, Denny. But we are here more to say, 'well done!'" We learned a Celtic song, heard amazing poetry, and participated in a section of the program where we all stood and sang along to one of Denny's favorite Abba songs.

Through the sharing, we learned about how Denny loved music. In her younger years, she was an opera singer who sang for the Queen, before having several debilitating surgeries. Her son James spoke about when Denny taught music and conducted a choir, she got the children to become aware of things in themselves they never knew were possible... to discover the spine-tingling sound which could come from only their voices, a sound that was uniquely theirs to share.

James said that even long after Denny stopped teaching singing and music, this continued to be her greatest joy – to get us to see things in ourselves anew, and to do things we weren't aware of that was possible.

The whole occasion was truly a remarkable honouring of a remarkable woman. We were experiencing laughter, some tears, and everyone left inspired – that we could each live a little more fully, and love a little more deeply.

After the funeral service, we gathered at her home enjoying stories and snacks on the lawn, under umbrellas in the gently falling rain. When the time felt right, I brought out Denny's graduation certificate to give to her daughter on her behalf.

As I spoke to the group which had gathered, I realised that Denny did not just graduate from the 100-Day course, she had also now graduated from this body, this life. I recognised that death, in a way, is like a graduation, and that Denny graduated with the highest honours. Her soul chose such a challenging path, and she met each challenge with a magnificent surrender into divine love.

Ancient Secrets Foundation, of which I'm a trustee… has been helping orphan kids for a long time. I was so happy to share with Denny's family that we have now named our operations for helping orphans, the "Denny Love Fund."

Denny herself was an orphan, who demonstrated for all of us that it doesn't matter where you come from, or what pain and trauma you have experienced in the past, but it is about what you do with it… and that the most difficult circumstances can turn into the most amazing miracles – when mixed with the divine ingredient of love.

One of my favorite teachers, Dr Naram, so beautifully said, "Any obstacle, challenge, heart-ache you may face, has within it the seeds of equal or greater benefit."

Denny was living proof of that.

What a great role model she is not only for the orphan kids, but for all of us as well.

Proceeds from this book go to help support the "Denny Love Fund". So you are also a contributing to the gift of love for these orphan kids, while at the same time benefiting yourself.

Thank you, Denny, thank you.

So how did Denny transcend beyond the dark and difficult experiences in her life, to bring such light?

What was the powerful tool she held, which was also able to touch so deeply the lives of others, including mine?

How can each of us 'graduate from life' with such distinction, like Denny?

I'm excited for you to discover as you read these pages...

"Love is the Only Truth"

Much love and respect,
Dr. Clint G. Rogers
Siddha-Veda Practitioner & Author of
Ancient Secrets of a Master Healer

Introduction

As I sit here, putting pen to paper, remembering my dearest friend, my soul sister Denny, known to me and many as Den, who sadly left this realm on the 19th of July, 2021, I realise how fortunate we were to have almost completed Den's dream of writing a book. So let me share a bit about Den and myself, and how this amazing book came about.

My name is Gill Wilkinson, I've been a therapist for over twenty-seven years, a mother to three children, all grown up, and Grammie to a beautiful grandson. I first met Den and her daughter Clare at a healing training course in Malvern, Worcestershire, England. Whilst drinking coffee and waiting for the course to start, there was a moment of instant recognition between us. We soon became great friends and I felt as though I had known Den forever. I would go and visit her in her Cumbrian home and eventually *Spirit* guided her to move down south, to Broadway in Worcestershire, which turned out to be five doors away from my home. And so, the adventures began, some of which we are sharing in this book. Over the coming years we continued our training, as well as focusing on our specialties: Den on her psychotherapy, hypnotherapy, Eden Energy Medicine (EEM) and healing, and I in reflexology, EEM, SCENAR and healing.

My greatest friend had a cup that was always half full. I have so much admiration and loving respect for how she coped with chronic pain, operations, heart attacks and slow loss of her independence.

Den worked with spiritual guides that she described as a group that she was once energetically a part of. It was decided between them that she needed to come back this time around. I felt very privileged to be able to connect with them, too. They would very often help me to help Den and help me along my spiritual path.

Den had so much wisdom that some called her the Wise One. When she transitioned, a shaman called her one of the Masters. She radiated love to all, she loved people and just spending time with her, you could feel quite uplifted. She had a direct phone line to *Spirit*, no ego in the way. She spoke truth and very often when you thought your situation or dilemma was complicated to work out, her answers could appear simplistic, which often made you wonder, "Why didn't I think of that?"

One of Den's wishes was to share as much wisdom and help with as many people as possible and that is how the book began. We wanted to present a mix of her life story, examples of how she worked and helped others, wise words and techniques that could help people on their journey, along with some very funny stories that happened.

Early in 2021, whilst taking part in the *100-Days Ancient Secrets* course with Dr. Clint G. Rogers, we got talking with him about sharing Den's wisdoms in a book. With his amazing help and under the umbrella of the Ancient Secrets Foundation, a team of volunteers from around the world was formed, led by Gen Brightlight.

I feel very honoured to have known Den for over twenty-eight years, my greatest friend, my soul sister, to have walked beside her, supporting her physically, sometimes emotionally, and mentally, whilst she helped me grow along my spiritual path – all mixed in with so much fun, love, laughter, friendship, and of course coffee and cake. To have been involved in creating this book, which we both were so passionate about wanting to do, is also an honour. I am very grateful to all those involved in helping to make this happen. Thank you from the depths of my heart.

With love from Gill and Dear Den,
who I'm sure is guiding me in this introduction.

PART ONE

Denny Dakin

June 15, 1940 to July 19, 2021

"How do you move
on from trauma?"

"This is an interesting question
because you never, ever,
really leave behind your story.
Your story is your life from
birth till you go home."

CHAPTER 1

My Story

I was born in June 1940 in London, in a place called Richmond. This is where my orphanage was. My mother was from an aristocratic family and she, along with my uncle and aunt, mixed socially with royalty. In those days having a baby out of wedlock was seen as appalling behaviour, so I was put up for adoption. I spent all of World War II there and didn't come out until I was six-and-a-half. But the horrors of my experiences in the orphanage coloured my whole life.

> *I was sexually abused the entire time I was at the orphanage by a group of three men. One man would come and take me, or one of the other two baby girls in my room, away with him. Initially, I was so traumatised I didn't remember this for many years.*

Spirit

I am very lucky because so much of the time when the real vile abuse was going on in the orphanage, *Spirit* took me out of my body, so I didn't actually physically have to go through the pain of what was being done to me. I was very definitely protected, by being lifted out and back to *Spirit*, which was so familiar and safe, it felt like home.

My Mother's Family

My grandfather was very much head of our family. He was behind the family having nothing to do with me. He couldn't get past the dismay, the anger, the shame, or whatever the emotions were in those days towards his beloved daughter and what she had done. When Grandfather died whilst at work at the Admiralty, my grandmother told Mother to get me out of the orphanage and bring me to 'St. Pees' (St. Peter's), which was the big school where Grandmother lived.

Young Denny

I was put on a train on my own. I was six-and-a-half, coming up seven, and I was stark staring terrified. There was a lovely lady on the train who realised how frightened I was, and she sat with me until we got to Maidenhead.

> *In my new life out of the orphanage, I went from sexual abuse to mental and emotional abuse. My grandmother treated me with shame and horror, though she did introduce me to music.*

Grandmother was a very clever woman. A very brilliant brain. Brilliant at history, math, and absolutely brilliant at music. She taught me to read and write music, even though we didn't have a piano. I adored music and that helped me tolerate the mad bits of behaviour where she could be utterly cruel and lock me in my room for no reason – trapping me – or giving me hell about something. I went from never knowing safety in the orphanage to mad behaviour at home.

My mother was like a nightmare. A nightmare that I stayed away from as much as possible. Looking back, I realise she was not a nasty person for the sake of being a nasty person, she was simply filled with emotional wounds.

> *Initially, my mother didn't know what went on in the orphanage because I didn't. I had buried it so deeply that I had absolutely no notion of what life had been, or if there had been a life other than the one I was living.*

There *was* one lady that came on the scene at 'St. Pees' who was without a doubt the most wonderful and remarkable lady that I met at that period of my life. Beth was the wife of my mother's brother, and she only lived about two hundred yards away. She saved my sanity from all my fears, upsets, and distress.

Aunt Beth even came to my rescue when, three years later, Mother married my stepfather. I was staying with Grandmother who, on the actual wedding day, had locked me in my bedroom so I couldn't be part of the wedding. My beloved aunt noticed that I was missing and rescued me. I stayed with my aunt and uncle while my mother and stepfather were on their honeymoon. There was such lovely kindness and understanding in Beth, without a spoken word. I was very lucky to have a magical person around me to help me keep going.

My Parents

After Mother got married, my life changed. I was introduced to my stepfather, and as far as I was concerned, he was nothing to me and I was nothing to him. The idea that I was going to share a house with him and my mother, who had a lot of the tendencies of my grandmother, was distressing.

We lived in a place called Tottenham Corner, near Epsom, my first home. My stepfather came into my life and was instrumental in giving me – teaching me – a foundation. It took him a long, long time because I didn't want anything to do with anybody. The patience, the love, the total freedom that this man gave me, allowing me to talk if I wanted to, and not if I didn't. There were no rockets. No lectures. He was just there.

My beloved stepfather slowly but surely introduced me to games with math involved. He started to do squares and patterns and play with numbers, which he played on a circular table we had in the sitting room. And I started to play with him.

I would have very little to do with *him*, but I would *allow* him, and that is a strange phrase, but I would allow him close enough to start playing some of his games because there wasn't an out-come. There was no demand. And unbeknownst to me, he was teaching me. And because of this, I was always top in the tests at school for all arithmetic and tables. I could give any answer so quickly and it was all centered on the games my stepfather taught me.

Everything was a game, there was no pressure, control, trying to boss or dictate. He just kept saying, "You are my daughter." And that was it. Bit by bit I learnt to trust. He always spoke the truth and if he couldn't speak the truth, he would say, "I can't talk about that one. You'll have to talk to your mother, ask her what she is thinking and why. But I am always here for you."

When my parents learned that I had been badly, badly abused in the orphanage, they responded with horror. Absolute horror! My beloved stepfather couldn't get past it.

Holidays with My Stepfather

Holidays in Cumbria, an area in the Lake District in the north of England, reminds me of fun and walking the fells with my father. By then, I didn't see him as a stepfather at all. He was my saving grace, I think, in the whole of my life, by his being there. His quietness, his fun, his no demands, but not taking fools softly – he was just a remarkable guy!

My father was great walking up the fells with because he would have the books with him – the famous sets of books of each climb, each walk, and each journey we made. And it was only years later that I found it rather ironic that I was the one who carried all the food and everything up the mountain and my father very kindly carried everything down when it was empty. But he had a way of putting that across where it never dawned on me that I was carrying the heavy stuff and he was carrying the light stuff!

One hilarious time, we were standing on the top of a misty fell. He was warning me about the patches of boggy areas, giving me a lecture about being careful, and knowing what to look out for. Then he set off and walked straight into a bog. Even he had the giggles because we had great difficulty getting him out.

> *When I later had children, I never left my children just with my mother; it was always with my stepfather there as well. Whether she realised, I don't know, but my stepfather was the one who I trusted with the children, because I trusted him.*

Spirit Hound

On another occasion I had a friend staying with us, and we were on top of a fell, and we saw, at the bottom of the fell, a car and two small children playing with the mother. We instantly assumed it was my mother with my two half-sisters, so we walked nearly all the way down, only to discover that we had completely the wrong car and children. We had a choice: carry on down to the bottom and take a twelve-mile road hike back to the car or go back up and down the next side.

We had done a whole day of walking and were tired. And remember, I had a friend who was also exhausted. He was not used to the fells. But as we started to go back up again, we were joined by a hound. The hound was magnificent in getting us back up to the top of the fell. She chased around us. She came back. She made sure we were all okay. She got us to concentrate our attention on her, rather than on our achy bones and how, "It wasn't fair!", which was a typical teenage response.

Well, we got to the top and found the correct way down, and the hound stayed with us to the bottom where my sisters and mother were with the car. It was decided that we would take the hound with us, which was very smelly, to the nearest police station to hand her in, because hounds were very valuable in the hound races.

Less than a week later father got the most wonderful letter saying, "Thank you so much." The hound had gone missing and was valued at over a thousand pounds! It was lovely that this hound had actually got us up to the top of a hill – or you could say *Spirit* set it up – but there was no way that we were going to get up without some help, and this hound appeared from nowhere and gave us just that.

We had lochs and rivers to swim in. Hills to climb. Birds, so lots of bird watching. We had horses that we rode. It was just bliss. They were special holidays!

My Music

I was in Yorkshire when I first met the piano. It was in a town called Marske and Father had just been made a senior teacher in one of those schools there. I had to go to a new school, and I was an unimpressed little 9-year-old girl, because I had loved the school I had attended before we moved.

A lady was standing by an open door and behind her was the most fantastic grand piano I had ever seen. I went straight to it, sat down, and proceeded to play. I just tuned in to the piano, the piano tuned in to me, and off we went. There was an absolute relationship. I hadn't actually played the piano before, but I knew my notes because of all my theory I'd been taught by my grandmother.

I was given permission to practice on this piano – to play her – and I loved it.

I read music better, I think, than I read words. And it was like they were there for me. They were in front of me on the piano and they just wanted to play. My love and my relationship with music was absolutely solidified by this phenomenal instrument.

My Sisters

When I was nearly nine, my sister Bron was born. I absolutely fell in love with her. That was the first time I met love. This little thing just produced an emotion in me. She was the most beautiful, glorious baby anybody could have, and she was *my* sister. I was going to look after this baby for all my life!

By the age of ten I had another sister, and life changed dramatically after that.

Whether I resented her, I don't really know. I don't really understand because my first sister I just adored. My second sister was very different and, I think, fairly ill. She slept in my parents' bedroom and had a special sort of nanny to look after her.

Whether that caused my problems, I don't know. But that is when my physical problems began.

Losing My Voice

We had moved to Newcastle-upon-Tyne where my father became headmaster of a school there. I loved school and got on well there, but within a week, my voice went. I ended up with absolutely no voice whatsoever. It got serious enough for my mother to take me to see the doctor, who directed me to a specialist to see what was causing this loss of voice. Obviously, it had to be psychological, as I could not produce a sound.

*In my memory of the orphanage, with the two other
little girls – we couldn't talk. We couldn't do anything. But we were in the same room, so we knew
everything that was going on to each of us – whose
turn it was to be taken – and that was when, initially,
I didn't say a word.*

The specialist at the hospital put me in a room with paper and
coloured pencils. I was asked to draw any picture I wanted, and
he'd come back in a while and see how I was doing. I drew a
tree and massive space. The tree was the only thing there, apart
from the sun, and me sitting underneath the tree.

*I was told a long time later that the specialist gave
one look and said, "She feels like she belongs
nowhere. She can't talk because there is no one
she can talk to." He said, "I am going to try an
experiment. I have got a little boy who broke his
left leg very badly, around his knee area. He can
walk perfectly well as it's all healed, but he's
decided he can't put his foot down and walk. He is
completely defeated mentally. I am going to put the
two of them together."*

The specialist had us walk up and down a corridor, giving us
each a set of instructions. To me: "The boy is an idiot. He can
walk perfectly well, but he has decided he can't, so he won't."
Obviously, the same thing had been said to him about me:
"She can talk perfectly normally, but she has decided she can't,
so she is an idiot." And this is how the two of us met. It was
very clever.

We hiked up and down this corridor with him throwing every insult he could at me. I just glared at his leg and then glared at him. And this went on for about three months. How our parents coped I do not know, but on this particular occasion he came out with something so ridiculously rude that I swung around, stamped my foot and said, "Who the hell do you think you are, talking like that?"

I completely got my voice back in sheer temper! He was so shocked that he had gotten a response from me, he put his foot straight down and started to walk. And between the two of us, we healed each other.

Developing a Stammer

Unfortunately, when I found my voice, I got a desperate stammer. Stammers run in our family, though I believe it is mostly on the men's side. But I had a really bad stammer. I remember the nightmare of trying to say something and not having the time to say it before the person had to move on. Or being given the word to speak, which wasn't the word I was after at all, and I ended up very, very distressed with this.

My parents found Mrs. Hutchinson, a most wonderful magical speech therapist, and she took me on. We didn't talk to each other, we sang. I could sing any sentence. I could sing anything and everything to her. Every time I tried to talk, I'd stammer, but Mrs. Hutchinson gradually got me to quote poetry, Shakespeare, and do the most extraordinary performances without a stammer, by singing it all. Any hint of a stammer when talking, I sang. I just sang a note, and the stammer went away immediately. Working with Mrs. Hutchinson set me on the path to becoming an opera singer. It was piano to start with, and then it became my voice.

Sports and Music

I had interesting teen years. I lived for sports and music. There was no time for anything else. I played hockey, golf, and swam for the county. The rhythm that I had in music was very beneficial for a game player. I had a wonderful Scottish pro who trained me, and he kept saying, "Denny, you've got to find a rhythm whereby you don't try and hit the living daylight out of the golf ball." So, I used Strauss as my rhythm, and it flowed.

Denny at University

Same with swimming. I was a natural back stroker and crawler and it was rhythm, rhythm, rhythm. I adored the training except when I felt thoroughly exhausted, which was regularly, but it was brilliant training, and our trainer brought our timing down miles. I loved representing the county, doing my best for the team; we had such fun.

When at university, studying singing, I ended up in a fabulous group of students who took me under their wing. We were there to support each other, when life was difficult, or we were having a bad music session with a teacher or something like that. It was extraordinary, and I loved the group. I loved the music. I loved the teachers. I was very spoiled by so many of them and so very, very lucky to be part of a marvelous collection of students and teachers at the same time and taught by them.

> *Here again is darling Spirit looking after this country bumpkin – being taken in by a wonderful group who protected the women, who saw that we all did as much as we could together.*

It wasn't till my late twenties that I became aware that there were men around. And they were trying to get my attention. I tried the occasional kiss and that was *urrrgggghhh*. I really was L-plated (Learner-plated) from the beginning to end. I was completely dumbfounded when men would go past and say, "Well, I would love to take you out for a drink." I would look at them, thinking, *"Is there something wrong with you? Why? You know, what is your point for going out for a drink?"* There was no romance in me, anywhere.

Opera

What happened with music and opera was one of the biggest heartbreaks of my life. I lived, ate, and slept music and opera. It was my life. I had won a scholarship to the Guildhall in London, which was a scholarship for opera and acting. I suppose you can say it involved tremendous studying and hard work. But to survive in any field of arts, you need to have a streak of toughness, with no disrespect to the outstanding singers throughout the world. I really struggled if I turned out to be better than someone else, because these were my friends, and that part of me didn't know how to respond.

I was doing well at Covent Gardens. I was singing in quartets, and once you have the whole sounds of the orchestra ringing through you, mixed in with the smells of the make-up, you just fly!

Then I Became Terribly Ill

I had an intussusception of my intestines (a part of the intestine slides into the other) and had to have a major operation. My bowel was actually turning inside out due to the damage from my abuse at the orphanage. It was the start of a long life of blockages.

> In those days, nobody had thought to really go searching when somebody had an intussusception at that age and was so ill. Nobody even thought of sexual abuse.

The operation interfered with my intercostal muscles (muscles that run between the ribs and help form and move the chest wall, which are vital for singers). I even wore a wrestler's belt to try and help support my singing. It didn't matter how hard I tried, I became what is known as a faulty singer. I started out as a dramatic soprano and became a lyrical soprano, with a light voice.

Another Operation

The final straw was yet another blockage. Again, this operation affected my intercostal muscles, and I was told by the Guildhall that they were sorry, but my voice wasn't the voice it used to be. My dream of a career as an opera singer had ended.

> *This made it difficult for me, but the main reason my career in opera finished was Spirit's decision to remove my ability to sing opera.*

Another Setback

The Guildhall suggested I take up an instrument, so I took up the classical guitar. I was with a fantastic Russian teacher for two years. She suddenly wanted me to travel with her for three years in America, studying and performing, as my light voice was blending beautifully with the guitar. But I said, "No." She was the one person I thought I'd say, "Yes" to. I'd have gone like a shot, but my *Spirit* said, *"No."* So I became the main accompanist for the top singers and became known more as an accompanist than I did as a singer in the end.

> *It's the clarity with which Spirit comes in when ego is full of 'yes,' and it is going to do this, and it sounds wonderful. It never crosses your mind that there is something else around the corner and in order to find that your Truth is saying, "Absolutely no."*

Meeting My Husband

I was almost thirty when I met Bob Dakin who would become my husband and father of my children.

It was through my parents at a county rugby match, and I remember thinking at the time how terribly rude and arrogant he was and had very little to do with him. So, I was very surprised when my father said, "Do come and sit down and join us," and, "Come back and have tea!" and everything else. I thought, *"This is strange,"* and thought no more about it. Life was far too interesting, with my swimming, sports, and music.

Denny as a young woman

It was a long time before Bob made it very clear that he was very interested in me as a person. And as a future wife. He was in the process of divorcing his first wife, who apparently didn't want children, and he did. It grew from there.

> I got the most extraordinary message from Spirit say-
> ing, "You ought to have his children." My response
> was, "I beg your pardon? What are you talking
> about?" That came very strongly. "You are having his
> children!" And that is exactly what happened.

Den with her kids when they are little

I didn't love Bob in that sense of love, which was one of my deep-seated learnings. But I did know that I was meant to have his children and, as a result, we got married. I had James first. When I was pregnant with James, my stomach stuck out so much, he appeared in the room before I did! But with Clare, she hid, very sensibly. She came into the world eventually, late.

> Both of my children had huge learning growths from their father and, of course, me, because I chose to be their mother and have his children. So, enormous learnings there. It all came to a crushing end due to his alcoholism, which started to damage the children.

Den with her kids when they are teenagers

The Joy of Teaching

I became a music teacher at a prep school for boys 8-to-13-years old. There was a lot of sport: rugby, cricket, and football. *"Music? Singing? Excuse me, what is that strange pastime?"*, seemed to be the reaction. It was during the period that the only boys singing were pop groups; it was not the 'in' thing to be in a choir!

I decided to train these youngsters as if music was the most natural thing in the world. You didn't have to know how to sing, you had to train the ear, not your voice. Gradually, music seemed to catch on and it seemed my way of teaching was unique – probably illegal, knowing me – I am very good at breaking rules if they don't fit!

Denny teaching swimming

I had a tough time, but bit by bit the boys began to love the games we played with singing. They all had to do little solos when it was their birthdays for the month, and I would suddenly bring in two parts and get half of them to sing one part and half to sing another part. If they couldn't find a note, then they sang out of tune. I turned it all into a great joke, calling every note they sang a planet. Middle C became 'Earth,' and that was home, and all they were trying to do was learn how to land back on planet Earth.

I started to give them the harmonies that I felt that would go with their voices, and from there this choir developed. When I found that some children couldn't really hit 'planet Earth,' I introduced them to hand bells. I taught them how to ring the bells and introduced harmonies for them to play, and they became unbelievably good!

We became good enough for people to notice and we got invited to do carol singing services and carol singing performances at all sorts of halls. The boys adored visiting care homes and the locals couldn't wait to see them. Parents started sending their children to the school for their music, and that was a tremendous honour!

> It was Spirit at its best. I was teaching and learning at the same time.

We entered competitions up against the Choir School just to see what we could do and to see if we were any good. Year after year, we would be in the first four places, which began to annoy the Choir School, as we were just *the* choir from *a* school.

On one of these occasions at this competition we'd already won five awards and we were being very quiet and sensible about it all. The final competition was an 'open' competition which meant anybody could enter for singing, for piano playing, or anything they wanted to do. I entered the hand bells group, and they were accepted.

They set off playing brilliantly. Suddenly, all lights went out and the hand bells just continued. They had rehearsed so much, they did quite brilliantly. By the time the lights came back on, they were still playing from memory and hadn't forgotten a single thing. There was tremendous applause for having achieved that with no lights, and they were promptly awarded as the winners.

The sheer delight of the joy of music and the ability to perform in any given situation. One boy had actually swung his bell too far and hit himself very hard on the forehead and had an egg which was a brilliant size. Nothing had stopped him one little bit from performing! Then to see our whole choir standing around this small group of boys who had won, it was one of the loveliest things I have ever seen. The joy from the choir to the boys with hand bells, who had also won something, and the hand bells' realisation that they were accepted and had been as good – if not better than the choir – which was developing quite a name, I have never forgotten that. The friendships that grew from there were wonderful!

Gill: It was Den's 80th birthday in 2020, and I proceeded to try and track down some of, as Den put it, 'The old boys,' that she taught nearly 40 years before. (Den didn't know anything about it.) I got in touch with about 20 'old boys' who absolutely loved Den to bits. We were trying to put together a video because we were in lockdown. I asked them if they would send a little short video or a photograph, and all 20 of them did something out of love for Den. It just shows you that after all this time, they still absolutely adored her. One of them said that it was the respect that she'd had for the youngsters that was mirrored back in all the boys. She had as much respect for them as they did for her.

Hypnotherapy

I had my first ever visit to an office offering psychotherapy and hypnotherapy in my thirties. The reason I was there was to find out why I was rolling my head and damaging my neck. My doctor had said I was harming myself. I knew I rolled my head when I slept, but I couldn't stop it. I came out of deep sleep into normal consciousness with my head rolling, and only then could I stop it. I was still doing it after I was married and had children. I met a delightful young therapist, newly trained, who was quite terrified to take me on as a case. Her boss was out, and she had just started.

My whole instinct – my own Spirit guide – just said, "She is the one you need."

With great trepidation I asked the young lady if she would work with me. She said she would have a go but was doing this without permission from her boss. And so we started on an eight-week course of therapy. It was her magic discovery, probably slightly unorthodox because it was so new, of an awareness that I had lived *elsewhere*.

I was suddenly shown a hospital, and my mother leaning over the bed trying very hard to smother me. She was interrupted by a nurse who obviously saved my life. The nurse took me and that is the last time I saw my mother. I was taken to the orphanage from there.

I Remember

Starting the hypnotherapy was the start of an incredible journey. A journey of *finding* the orphanage, *seeing* the orphanage, and then gradually feeling the anguish and the pain, and witnessing these two wonderful little girls, my great friends. I was thrown by the fact that my mother had tried to kill me at birth, which somehow didn't surprise me, but I had to get used to this new awareness.

I urgently tuned in and tried to find the two girls from the orphanage using my psychic skills. I thought they were dead by then. A few years later I became very distressed. I knew it had to do with the orphanage. I felt another layer of emotions coming up within me that needed to be looked at.

I contacted a wonderful therapist, who is also a shaman, who told me to get down to see her and, "Let's sort it out." So, Gill took me down to see her.

Lucy and Mary

The first thing we learned was that one girl, a woman by then, had died the week before.

We discovered the horrendous damage from the orphanage days had affected them both. Lucy and Mary were both alcoholics. Lucy had died from a drug overdose and Mary from suicide. I felt an immense guilt that I had got out of the orphanage and left them behind.

My therapist helped to heal that wound and brought our essences together. She found the girls' Spirits very easily; they were very close. She brought the three of us together into the harmony that made us able to relax with each other. To forgive and forget. To honour, to respect, and to understand. It was a tremendous breakthrough for me to be able to relax and know that they were okay now.

The Orphanage

Many people ask me whether I ever went back or tried to find or report the orphanage. I did nothing whatsoever. I had no desire to go anywhere near it! But an interesting fact: When I was studying opera, I had digs in Finchley Road, which I discovered was where the orphanage had been. Remember at that time I had no memories of the orphanage days. I mean, of all the places to live!

My Trauma

People ask me how I have coped with all the physical trauma and survived what has gone on in my life.

How the Body Copes

If one goes through the physical damage, to start with, or through what has happened with my life, and the abuse in the orphanage in particular, the physical body will understand the trauma.

My body suffered the pain, where Spirit very kindly removed me from my body and had me up with Spirit. But after the abuse, when I came back into my body, I was aware of extreme pain.

Hearing The War

I spent all of World War II in the orphanage in London, but I don't remember any of the war sounds, which I find very interesting. After the war, I witnessed people's reactions to hearing bangs and sounds like that; one could see people walking on the road and suddenly drop flat to the ground, in sheer shock from memory of what they had been through during the war. I remember being very worried as to why people were lying down and getting up in an embarrassed sort of way.

No Tears

All my life I have had great, great trouble crying. Over the years my daughter chased me, saying how important it was to cry. I think my inner child wasn't taught how to cry; she was taught to be silent.

> *At the orphanage we didn't have language really to start with, we were too young. But with the treatment that we were handed, you didn't cry.*

One day I had an interesting realisation. I went into my silence and was looking back, and all of a sudden, I had this picture in my mind:

> *I was back in the orphanage and I heard these ghastly footsteps. We all knew what the footsteps meant. The man was coming to collect one of the three of us. It turned out to be my turn and when I was picked up by him, part of me inside absolutely froze. I was smiling. I could see what I was doing. The others knew exactly what was going to happen,*

but I had bile coming right up through my whole stomach, throat, everywhere, and it was hidden behind a smile.

I used to smoke, and when that realisation showed me that my smoking was a cover up for the bile, I instantly stopped smoking. How extraordinary is that? After that I could cry a little, but I'm sure not as much as my daughter would have liked. Gill always senses when I need to cry and asks me if it's time to watch *Les Miserables,* as I always cry when I watch it!

The Trauma Continued

Twenty plus years ago, I had tremendous pain in the body over a period of months. The diagnosis eventually came through: rheumatoid arthritis (a long-term auto-immune disease that primarily affects the joints). It was right through my body on every level and crippling me totally.

Gill: Despite over several years exploring all avenues, Denny's rheumatoid arthritis never went into remission. It badly affected her joints, muscles, and bones, which affected her mobility. She was in constant pain and as the disease affected her more and more, I knew without any doubt that I would step up and support her as best I could.

Moving on from My Trauma

How do you move on from trauma? The emotional impact of it is basically what moves, more than anything else.

Moving Away from Ego

Your learning moves you away from your ego, the blame game, the accusations, and the 'poor me.' All these ego emotions that we are all brilliant at get highlighted to be looked at.

The Common Denominator

I realised that there was *one common denominator* throughout each of my experiences, regardless of what I was experiencing. I was the common denominator.

Gradually I understood that if I was the common denominator, then the players around me were playing roles for me to learn from. That was a very big pill to swallow. Could all this horror I experienced in the orphanage possibly be for me to learn from? Yes. *Spirit* had asked me to explore and experience all of this to see if I could move beyond the need of the agony in my physical, mental, emotional, and spiritual levels.

The Journey Is Me

My *Spirit* showed me that everybody in the plays is on their own journey, and those that chose to help me in my learning played the roles they were asked to play. From that, they will either have their own karma or whatever their journey is all about, but that has nothing to do with me.

Every one of us is on our own personal journey, and the journey that one is being asked to remember and move back to is very simply that *everything is love*. I'm not talking about the 'ego' love that has strings attached, or love of partner or parent, or love of this, love of that. Unconditional love is a different love.

Unconditional Love

I started realising about unconditional love and how to grow, by loving everything. When you start to unconditionally love all those people who damaged you – who created physical pain that you live with all the time – *and you love them and understand* that they are on a journey, and there is no blame game, it is just acceptance and unconditional love.

Denny

When I really understood what "loving self" meant – slipping away the concerns of what I looked like physically and mentally, and what people thought of me, or how I wanted to be represented – it was an enormous shift of awareness that centered around learning to love all that I am and letting go of ego.

Yes, it took some work, but once I had shifted into loving myself, my ego got bored. It didn't have an audience because I no longer fed into my ego. My ego was not getting the feedback it wanted, so suddenly I found I was doing something totally different, and it was so much more beautiful and wonderful!

These Days I Have Moved on to a Place of Love

- There is no blame game, or poor me, or how damaged I am. There is no ego.
- It comes from my truth, my *Spirit*, who is showing me that everybody in the play is on their own journey.
- Those who chose to help me in my learning played the roles they were asked to play, but that is nothing to me.
- I have learnt how to take ownership for every event that has happened in my life, because I am the common denominator.
- The journey is me.

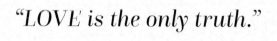

"LOVE is the only truth."

"I was always connected to Spirit and grew up knowing my connection. As I got older, I understood more and more and talked to my guides. And as I developed with this knowledge, I started receiving information not just for myself, but for others too."

CHAPTER 2

Spirit & Spirit Guides

What Is Spirit

We are *Spirit* sent back into human form. So often people think they are humans having a Spiritual experience, which is back to front. If you get it the right way round – that we are *Spirit* having a human experience – we can begin to understand.

When Did Spirit Appear?

Spirit was aware that it was a very tough learning and chose to be involved during my early age. When I was young, I could leave my body effortlessly to be with *Spirit*. I did this with great regularity, until *Spirit* decided that as an adult, this was not the outcome *Spirit* was looking for. The outcome was to stay in my body, understanding that love is down here, but also up there. In actual fact, love is within me.

Spirit would never leave me, wherever I was. But I had to learn to stay in my body and become love *from within* the body.

I feel one of the main reasons *Spirit* wanted me totally in my

43

body is this journey I am on. I am being asked to explore and experience these emotions, and as I travel through each level of learning, I get closer and closer to this wonderful feeling of love.

Why Spirit Chose This Life for Me

I can only assume that *Spirit* decided that it could gain a great amount of emotional learning at a very deep level, with severe pain, to see if my humanness – my ego – could eventually work with my *Spirit* and begin to understand the reason for the journey, which was to grow beyond the need of blame game, pain, suffering, and fear.

We are sent back into human form, which entraps us in our body, for us to learn through emotional learning and understand why we have that emotional learning, and what we need to change about us to stop that experience happening again.

We experience our lessons through our ego, in an ego body, which is the lowest level of intelligence. It's doing its best to keep us safe, but sometimes it is unable to move beyond an experience.

For example, we may be thirty-five years old, but this learning could have a horrific effect on our inner five-year-old, and we have an instant response from the five-year-old and how she dealt with it, not how the thirty-five-year-old would deal with it. The learning is to understand that repeat pattern, how our ego responded saying, *"No, I'm not doing it that way. I shall deal with it as a thirty-five-year-old would today."* The energy then shifts, and you are looking at the learning through the eyes of an adult.

Every element that is in our ego was in my life. It was learning to gradually move beyond living in those emotions, to realising this is just a story and that you can take out the blame game and the emotional reactions and just look at it.

It really is the start of becoming one with all that we are, loving everything we are, from warts on the feet to pain in the body. Our body still needs love. It didn't ask for the pain or warts, so it's our ability to say, *"I am so sorry"* and send it love.

Bit by bit over many, many years, the realisation started to come in that here was the reason for living. It was to be the best that I could be for the *Spirit* that I really am.

One of the workshops Gill and myself ran was called: *Who am I? What am I? Why am I?*

These are important areas to look at in one's life and remember:

- You are actually *Spirit* here on this planet!
- You are exactly what you are meant to be.
- You are learning the correct learnings that your beloved *Spirit* wants you to learn.

It shows the wonderment of you. It also shows the incredible bruising of a lot of your journey and the ego pain that accompanies it. If you take away all the emotion, we are simply being asked to move beyond the need of undermining or blaming ourselves; of being ashamed or disrespecting ourselves. And turning it around to, "I am beginning to understand I am still as pure and beautiful as when I came in, and I shall go home beautiful, exactly the way I came in."

Spirit Sends a Strong Message

I had suffered from a serious back injury at the prep school by catching a boy falling out of a tree. He was perfectly alright, bless him. Eight years old. Quite a large child. He had just lost his balance and fell and I happened to be standing in exactly the right position. I put my hands out and caught him and I tore up both sides of my back. The results were a bit grim as I spent many months lying on the mattress in our bedroom.

I just lived on the mattress on the floor, which was the only place I could sit or lie down. Gradually, I was able to get up and about again but with great care. I could do very little and, of course, managed to hurt it yet *again*, totally accidentally, while in my home in Carlisle, Cumbria.

Eventually I got to see a neurologist. My parents took me, as I was in a wheelchair. I had x-rays and when I saw the consultant, he asked me a few questions. Then in a sarcastic voice he made comments that triggered my temper, and I gave him a mouthful in response. I swept out in my wheelchair and that afternoon I wrote him a letter saying how rude he was.

Two days later I received a call from the consultant who said, "I'll take you on." He added, "I just needed to see that you are a fighter because what we have to do is not funny. I can't guarantee an operation, as it's so dangerously close to the spine. But there will be some experts there and we are going to try and see what we can do."

Then *Spirit* joined in. I was in bed and suddenly there was bouncing on my bed. At first, I didn't know what it was. My duvet was fine. Everything seemed fine. But there was something going on, on top of my duvet, bouncing and being annoying, trying to get my attention. It took me a while to realise it was my *Spirit* crowd demanding my attention and saying, "Go and have the operation!"

My *Spirit* guides kept on bouncing on my bed until I went to the hospital. In a fit of anger and pain I yelled, "Okay! I've heard!

I understand! I'm going to have the operation." In response I had triple the amount of bouncing just to acknowledge that they heard me. It calmed down after that. They've never bounced on my bed since.

My *Spirit* guides connected a lot and helped me realise I had to slow down as part of my learning. I was desperate to do things with my children and I was also teaching in the prep school. They were teaching me to live more in the now and pay more attention to what my *Spirit* guides were saying.

My Spirit Guides

I have always had guides, right from the word go. Guides know what is going on. They wrote the stories, and they are there to help us. We can hear them. Just be still, open and get ego out of the way.

The energies can be in any shape or no shape at all. They are me, but in different guises, with incredible wisdom, and of course there is no ego. Ego doesn't exist. It's an understanding that experience has been chosen by my *Spirit* and I am doing my best to cope with it. This of course applies to each of us along our journey.

I Am Captain

I am basically captain of the crew. The body is my crew. It's doing its best to keep me going and I am blaming it, like so many people. They'll say, "Oh, my back is gone again." I'll stop and say to them, "So your back asked to go? No, it didn't. Take responsibility for your back. What have you done for this to happen? Maybe it's being stressed or that programme is running in your body that your poor old back has gone. An emotional programme repeating, *I can't cope anymore. I can't take the stress.*"

It doesn't matter which part of your body is carrying that particular learning curve, that part of your body will let you know. If we then can respond with great love and say, *"I am so sorry I haven't been paying attention, but well done me! I have seen what I have just been doing and I am so sorry."*

The more we start taking responsibility and look at the common denominator – me – then it is my story, nobody else's. It is *Spirit, Spirit* guides, and it is our beloved *Spirit* that is our essence and never anything else.

Guides Disappear

What was unexpected was that my first guide, who was male, just disappeared and was replaced by a female guide. My new guide was very definitely feminine energy and quite a strict teacher. It took a long time, with me looking for my old guide, to begin to understand that the standard of the old guide had been reached by my development. I was equal in learning with the first guide. Therefore, they changed that guide to a guide more advanced than I was to help me with my learnings.

Every time I reached a set point in my development, a new guide would appear, until I was joined by a group of guides. I got to know them tremendously well. I learned you can love them. And each time this shift happened, I had the ability to pat myself on the back and go, *"Well done! You have reached another milestone of learning because they have gone and, in their place, here is the next level of learning!"*

In other words, as I reached that level of Spirituality, understanding, knowledge, and how I was living my life that was at the standard of that particular guide, I became him or her.

We move to the level of a Spirit who is helping our growth. Once we have grown to that level, that Spirit

*becomes us, and another more mature advanced
Spirit comes in.*

Guides Become One

One of my biggest upsets was the day my guides disappeared.
We had been working so well together for about two years and
I think I wailed, "Come back! All of you! I don't want this!" It
was one of my senior guides that said, *"You are the standard now.
We can't teach you anything."*

I remember calling back, "What about friendship? What
about love?" I was learning all about these through them. The
reply was, *"You get that in real life. You don't need to search for these
emotions and characters that are not in reality."*

In fact, the group of guides and myself had all merged together
and we'd become one.

When I lost my first guide, I did not lose my first guide, we
became one.

Forever Connected

Some of my guides definitely are not me, they are my teachers.
But I am connected as much today, if not more, than I was as
a tiny child. I can talk to them just like talking to my beloved
friend Gill. Our conversations are that kind of level, there is no
sort of holier than thou, because I am always with them, we are
like one. I am never alone.

As I grew older, I never lost connection. I could call upon them
whenever I needed. I still can, and still do, except that now I very
rarely have to call upon them because I feel part of them. We
are one wonderful group of love and different aspects of myself.
That has never ever changed. I don't really call upon them, they
just seem to turn up. I could be saying something – thinking it's

really quite intelligent – and they could cut me straight off and come in with something that is far more pertinent and random, which would never have crossed my mind.

Gill: Den was occasionally allowed to float out from her body, but only when I was giving her a treatment, usually reflexology, because I held her energy. It was as though we were attached by a cord. When I finished her treatment, I slowly brought her back. Den felt it was quite a treat to be allowed by *Spirit* to go floating off. We usually had a great conversation afterwards, me sharing what I discovered working on her. That could be anything from her crowd of guides chatting to me or discovering something on one of her energy levels or something physical through her feet, whilst Den might be sharing which planet she visited, or which guides were around, and sometimes words of wisdom for her or both of us.

Joining the Spiritual Community

When I was still living up in Cumbria there was a Mind, Body & Spirit show going on. I wasn't going to go, but Zoe, a beloved friend of mine (like an adopted daughter), wanted to go to the show. I said I'd go with her in the day but not to the evening event, which was being run by the Spiritual Church with different healers and mediums. I was adamant on that!

We went to the afternoon show, and after I said goodbye to Zoe I was sitting down to my supper. I looked at the clock, and seeing it was 7pm, I thought, "Ah, the evening presentation must be well underway and the access to the upstairs hall will be closed now. Perfect."

Suddenly, I got such a strong feeling from inside me that I put my knife and fork down. I thought, *"What on earth?"*, and I found myself being got up and propelled round to the back door with my car keys. In my utterly stubborn Denny way, I was saying, *"I am not going to this event!"*

I literally was ejected from my own home and found myself driving to the venue. I knew I wouldn't be able to get in because there is a lift that takes you upstairs and that would be closed. Plus, I knew there wouldn't be anywhere to park due to such a small parking area.

Of course, there was a parking place right by the door! I could feel the struggle with *Spirit*, and I could feel my anger rising, absolutely fed up with being chased like that. I got out of the car to walk over to the gentleman standing by the entrance, waiting for him to say, "I am terribly sorry, the event has started. You can't go in now." But not a bit of it.

One of the Spiritual teachers – mediums – was late and so nothing had started. Everybody was waiting for her to arrive. So where did Denny find herself? In the lift, going up to the floor. The speakers were all there, except this one medium who hadn't arrived. Dressed all in blue, I sat in the back and, I must say I was hiding, pretending I wasn't there.

Suddenly, the door opened, the lift had arrived and, full of apologies, this delightful lady came in. There was a short explanation of what was going on and what was going to happen. We had a little prayer and then we just sat in silence to see who wanted to start.

One of the mediums started first and chatted away, speaking to one or two people. I was completely disenchanted. The arrogant behaviour of mine! I was bored and wanted to go. I remember looking at the clock thinking, *"How much longer have I got before I can get away at half time?"*

Suddenly the lady who arrived late stood up and said she wanted to talk to the lady dressed in blue. I was paying absolutely no attention in the back. She politely repeated, "This is very unusual, but I need to speak with a lady all in blue." Some of the audience turned around and pointed to me. Through gritted teeth I said, "I think you might be referring to me." With a wonderful smile, she said, "Yes, it is you." Then she continued.

"My session tonight is all about you and is all to do with you. Welcome!" She went into a whole series of stories about me that were totally true! I was sitting up feeling acutely embarrassed. My ego was running rampant, and I was suddenly listening, because this woman knew about me.

She asked, "Have you lost children?" "No," I replied. "I have got two, but never lost any."

"Well, I have got two children from the *Spirit* world who are in your house every day sitting as if they are watching television."

"This is true," I said. "I know them. They are there, but nobody can see them except me. And they have been there for ages. They just turn up, are happy, and leave when they are ready."

She talked about them, and then she talked about me. And by the time she had finished, I just wanted to crawl into a hole. Thankfully, there was a half time.

I got surrounded by four mediums, who all wanted me to join their spiritual churches. They said I had a spark, a special light, and a vision, and they could help me develop. The whole of my body was saying, *"Absolutely no!"* So, I said, "Thank you very much but no thank you. This is not my path. As far as I am concerned, I wasn't meant to be here tonight."

The lady medium who had spoken to me turned around and said, "My dear lady, you were the only person that was supposed to be spoken to tonight."

We reiterated that I had done everything I could to *not* be there, and *Spirit* had outwitted me – lovingly, charmingly, sweetly, and with my ego jumping with anger. I had to acknowledge that the behaviour of *Spirit* had been quite brilliant.

I didn't join any of the spiritual churches because I knew I wasn't meant to. But it was such an insight to discover that others could see essence the way I could!

She was the only person ever that knew about these *Spirit* children that sat in my lounge.

I have no idea who they were. They didn't need me to know, just needed to be loved and given safety. It was one of those extraordinary experiences that come into your life. Something really strange happens, and that strangeness becomes part of you. I found it all very, very fascinating, and very discombobulating at the time.

The Séance

I was invited to a séance and was asked if I would go to balance out the numbers with a group of people that apparently did séances quite regularly. The organiser had lost her grandmother and wanted to make connection. Now, I had never been to a séance in my life. I was doing my own work, and not with this side of life at all. But I agreed as I didn't have to do anything, plus I might learn something.

The evening came and my friend gave me a lift. We arrived and there were about ten of us around this massive table in the kitchen. There were letters all the way around the table, and a glass in the middle, and that was it. They were all chatting and talking. I didn't know any of them, except my friend. I didn't know the lady whose house we were in either.

We all sat down, and I was asked if I understood what was going on. "Not really." All I knew was that we were trying to get the grandmother to come through and talk.

We all had to put our fingers on the glass and stretch madly backwards and forwards across the table. Then, all of a sudden, the glass moved off on its own. I wasn't paying any attention because my arm was hurting at this point.

The woman started calling out letters and somebody wrote them down. It spelled out who they wanted to make contact with. The person was somebody the group didn't know called 'Den.'

"Ha!" I said, "That is me. That is my name. I am Den or Denny."

She said, "Right. Say hello. Talk." But I didn't know this person and she said, "Just talk. They have connected to you."

I said, "Well, it is a male. He lives in America. He is from a long, long, long time ago and he is delighted to meet one of the family." I added, "The name doesn't mean anything to me. I don't know a Michael."

I fumbled along like that, going, "I am so terribly sorry. I am not getting any other clues, other than he and his brother moved to America." I didn't get any surname or anything that helped. So, I had to say, "I can't take it any further." The owner of the house said, "Okay, let's cut the séance off and let's start again and see where we go this time."

We all took a breath and off we went again, and I thought, *"This is an interesting evening, I wonder how long I can last,"* as I was feeling embarrassed due to not being able to give any information about who had come through.

Anyway, to cut a long story short, every time we started the séance – which must have been seven or eight times – every time it was someone for me! After the eighth time I offered to sit out. But this didn't work either. With a groan from the lady of the house, she said, "The glass won't do it without you, let's try it just one more time."

Guess what? Yes, it was for me. We stopped the séance after that, with me leaving very rapidly, hugely apologising.

Now, to take this story on to what really matters. It's about a week later. I am down with my parents for an evening, and I am casually chatting about my experience, not thinking anything much about it, and waiting for one of them to say, *"What a load of rubbish,"* when my beloved stepfather goes and gets the family tree from my grandmother's beautiful antique desk. We start checking the names and discover that *all of the names* from the séance are on my family tree!

I was more shattered at that point than I had been all evening at the séance. Just thinking how weird that my stepfather had found all these people who had connected with me.

The More You Learn the Less You Know

This is a very interesting point I've discovered in my life. *Spirit* will allow you to see a lesson or understand a lesson when it decides that the ego – the human, the brain – can cope with the shock of the learning. What went on in the orphanage is a very good example of not having to handle it until I was able to handle it.

It's only when we have the knowledge that we can have a breakthrough. You go from being completely stuck in a particular area for no seeming reason other than the fact that you just don't get the answer, to suddenly getting what it is you've been searching for.

It arrives from nowhere through a different picture. You've done something different, but you don't know what. You can't repeat it to get the whole thing, and in comes consciously what it is you've just understood. It's a lovely breakthrough and you go, "My goodness, it's all to do with that?"

You are able to work with it, and be with it, love it, learn to love it, and empathise. What I discovered, too often, is a wonderful hurdle appears – a lovely bit of learning – and then all of a sudden *Spirit* decides, "Oh, jolly good, yes, she is not doing too badly. I am going to put a whole lot more learning steps in." And I get landed with three or four learnings – curves, is what I call them – where I come into scenarios which I haven't dealt with very well. And they are there for me to *actually deal* with. And they keep pointing to what I have just succeeded with and are trying to bring in a comparison of some sort. Not very easy! This is quite an interesting way of *Spirit* helping you clear your own backyard.

> *I have done all this growth learning to the best of my ability, on behalf of Spirit. I will do so till my dying breath, and hope that somewhere along the line I have carried out some of Spirit's wishes in my muddled way.*

"We move to the level of a Spirit who is helping our growth. Once we have grown to that level, that Spirit becomes us, and another more mature advanced Spirit comes in."

"I had an extraordinary experience when I was in hospital. It started me down the path of training to be a therapist by building on my natural talents with channeling and being psychic."

CHAPTER 3

Finding My Calling

Becoming A Therapist

My life-changing experience was witnessed by a senior woman doctor who was in the ward with us all, having had her leg amputated.

I couldn't get out of bed because I had so many tubes in me. One day, a beautiful little old lady, who had a dark, awful energy, was admitted to the same ward. It turned out, this sweet lady – so innocent, so gentle – had cancer. The daughter came back with the lady's suitcase and left. It seemed the daughter had told her that she couldn't possibly look after her, that she wasn't coming home and would have to go into a cancer hospital to die! The little old lady quietly wept.

That night I dreamt that I got out of bed, leaving all the tubes behind, and went to the bed of the little lady to sing "Ave Maria" to her. I did something with my hand, but I have no idea what. I do remember the "Ave Maria," and the clarity and the pureness of it. Nothing moved, nobody came into the ward. When I finished, there was a loving light. This woman so desperately needed to be held and loved.

When I finished what I'd been asked to do, I found myself walking back to my bed, getting into the bed, and reconnected to the tubes. And then I went to sleep. *What a strange dream!*

In the morning, the doctor who'd had her leg amputated came up in a wheelchair. She had a piece of paper, which she had written on, and put it very gently down on my bed.

"Denny, last night I was awake the entire time, it seems for a reason," she said. "I have written the reason. I want you to read it. But read it quietly and carefully."

"Oh, thank you very much," I said and tucked the paper away. That night, when it was all peaceful, I read it.

She had witnessed the entire event. It wasn't a dream. It had actually happened!

The letter said that this was my future, my life. I was there for people; I was there for love. And to be honest, I freaked, because to me this had been a dream, not reality. I couldn't believe what she had seen, what she had witnessed. But she wouldn't know my dream. She witnessed this!

> *It took two years for me to then go, "I have got something to do here. I am now ready to do it." And so I began my journey studying therapy, psychotherapy, healing, and Eden Energy Medicine.*

Carrying the World

Many times, I have been told that I am carrying the world energetically. I don't think it is a solo thing. What I do know from my world that I have been shown and told, is that I'm also made to watch that the work I am doing, and the learning I am doing, embraces the work that others are learning and doing.

I am the overall healer of that situation.

I take on their emotions, their difficulties, as mine. I help them release, but often at the expense of my own learning. I know there are others out there doing the same. How many others have been asked to carry the world's pain, I don't know. But I do know that I have done it for very many years, and I believe I have helped change the level of pain and emotion that is going on at the time, so it's more manageable and can be worked through.

Travelling When I Sleep

I travel when I sleep and go where I am sent to help those in difficulties. I don't choose any of this, and I am able to ask my beloved essence, my *Spirit*, when I am really tired, *"Please, no work tonight,"* to allow me to have a restful sleep. Which *Spirit* very kindly does.

If anyone finds they have been asleep and wake up extremely tired, perhaps that means that they have been busy working in their sleep or travelling in their sleep. If you are travelling at night, my suggestion is to remember that you are in partnership with your essence.

It's knowing you can say at bedtime, *"I don't want to travel. I don't want to do any work tonight at all. I would like, please, just to sleep and regain energy,"* and you will be heard and acknowledged. And you will be left alone all night. As long as you are firm, and you are truthful and honest in what you are requesting, you will get it.

Kundalini Experiences

They were amazing experiences. I don't know how or why they happened, but I had three and they were all quite fascinating. I had no idea how you move out of your body into a kundalini experience, but my first just seemed to happen.

One: I was part of a world, as air and the wind. I could see and feel everything. Initially, I did panic a bit because I felt lost, as I didn't know where I was. But along with constant conversation with guides and other energies, there was a wonderful sensation of freedom, love, peace, and joy. The colours were amazing, and everything was very clear and bright. It was beautiful and I basked in it all.

But when I arrived back, if that is the correct phrase, I just wept and wept, because whatever had happened, it so moved me that I didn't want to come back. I just wanted to stay in that amazing place. The distress in me was very profound, but life carried on.

Two: A number of years later, I had another kundalini experience. I was lying in bed in a light meditation, and I was taken straight up into a world where there were other activities going on. There were corridors and rooms made of clouds, and yet they were proper rooms. Some of them were work rooms. It was a complete avenue I was taken down, looking at the skills being trained and the activities going on in this complex.

I remember one distinct experience I can only describe as an electricity shop. There were two workers there who were very welcoming. They were endeavouring to create electricity working with just their hands. They just needed to touch something and light would be there! But what staggered me was it was so simple, and it worked brilliantly. They so enjoyed what they were doing, and it took so little to make it work.

Luckily, I wasn't so tearful this time, but I realised I couldn't stay because I was out of my body. In a deep way I began to accept the fact that I was being shown what could happen in the future, what was possible if we all worked to create this simpler way of living.

Three: This experience happened with the passing of my beloved stepfather. He was, as far as I was concerned, my life saver and I adored him. We were in a hospice because he was 'going home.' He had kidney failure, and he was lying there. It was my mother and I on duty. We treated him as if he were awake with us and played games and talked around him.

I decided to get us both some coffee and was in the kitchen when a very strong voice said, *"Go back."* I asked, *"Can I make the coffee?"* and the answer was, *"No, go back."* I went straight back, and Mother was sitting holding Father's hand. I said, "I have been sent back, not sure why, but I haven't got a drink yet."

I sat down and within seconds the room changed. It just became full of all the most wonderful energies of past family and friends. Amongst them all was my beloved sister Bron, who had died a number of years earlier from myeloid leukemia. I just sat and watched, and I suddenly saw this spark of electricity – electromagnetic energy move from Father up into Mother's arm and disappear.

He had gone, but he had gone surrounded by huge love and just adored by those waiting for him as well. My other sister and her husband arrived literally two minutes too late. The decision was I would go home and prepare the house for when Mother came home. As I got into the house, all I could hear was laughter, singing, joy, and love! Such fun going on and in the middle of it, I kept hearing my father's voice going, *"Oh! Oh! Oh!"* with surprise. He had never been a believer in anything, and there he was like a small child being led round and witnessing those around him, and the love of him, and I was able to be part of it all.

It was just a wonderful farewell party, with my father still saying, *"Oh!"* at the end. I have never ever forgotten the beauty of that.

There was no separateness. I could hear and receive and send out. I was like the wind. I picked up every message that was floating and delivered it where it was supposed to be. Everything had conversation, universal language. Nothing was silent unless it chose to be. Everything was alive and thriving and talking about themselves. I realised how far behind we all are on our planet, in comparison to what they were able to do.

Finding Lost People

This came about because a friend contacted me. One of her friends was on holiday abroad and her daughter went missing. The daughter wasn't bipolar, but something similar, and needed great caring for. The family reached out to ask if I could help.

Whilst my friend thought of the young woman, I tuned in. I saw her in water. She was lying in the middle of a type of pond. This led to the police finding her.

The police then contacted me and came for a chat. It seems they used the psychic abilities of people they trusted to help find those missing. So, over a period of two years, I helped them.

I was asked to look for somebody last seen sitting on a wall just outside the back entrance of a pub. It was a rural pub and just across the road from the pub there was a bridge with a stream. I tuned in and first thing I saw was the body. I then realised that I had seen *another* body! It was further along under the tunnel.

I remember ringing the police, feeling horribly sick and telling them I'd found two bodies. Sure enough, they knew both the people because they had been locals, and they obviously had come to harm in some way coming out of the pub.

I was really ill, and Spirit came in with a vengeance and sat down beside me, saying, "This stops now!

*This is not your future work. We stop it now!" I had to
ring up the police and tell them this was making me ill.
It was a horrible, horrible experience!*

Past Lives

Many years ago, I was attending a course run by a wonderful guy.
We had been asked to tune in and see what we'd been before our
present life. After all the group talked about the people they'd
been, it was my turn, and I knew I had to speak my truth. "I
had been the wind."

I discovered I have the same gifts today. The wind sends out
and receives and passes on. In this lifetime I receive information
and share everything. I receive, and I give out.

Best Workshop Ever

I had been asked to run a workshop in London for a day. There
were about 150 to 200 people offering many different therapies,
and to be honest I didn't know what half the therapies were that
they were doing. But it didn't seem to matter, they were there to
learn from me how to be the best therapist they could be.

The morning went well, we did extraordinarily well. I learned
a heck of a lot as I was getting some of them to act out their
therapies, and I was getting paid for it! We did a lot of hard work,
and we then broke for lunch.

When we came back from lunch you could see many wanted
time out. Some wanted to go to sleep or rest, and they struggled
to concentrate. I started to talk. I was talking about how much
they respected, valued, and loved their bodies and told them we
were going to go through the physical, mental, emotional, and
Spiritual levels. I suddenly realised that two thirds of them were
more asleep than awake.

With a chuckle inside of me, I knew how I was going to stir them.

I asked them if they were happy with their physical state. They answered, "Yeah, yeah, everything was fine." You could tell there was this thought of, *"Please get on with it. We want to do something else."*

So, I said, "I am asking you again, to check that you are all blissfully happy about your physical state in any given scenario."

"Yes, yes, yes, no trouble there at all."

I said, "That is absolutely wonderful! So, for the rest of this workshop, you can all strip off and do it *noodles*."

You have never seen therapists cover up so fast! The men banged their legs together; crossed them. The women sat up and pulled their clothes around themselves. It was a comedy act and I didn't say a word.

They witnessed themselves and they started to laugh, and they suddenly began to see where I was coming from, and I was saying "You have managed to lie to yourselves effortlessly because you are all beautifully covered in your clothes. I say take off your clothes, and the whole of your system goes into triple shock because it has never been asked to do anything like that or tell the truth."

We then had probably the best workshop I have ever run because we went through the physical, mental, emotional, and Spiritual levels of how their bodies were dealing with everything that was going on, and how much hurt they have had and how much pain. They off-loaded so much; it was wonderful to see! It probably was the best workshop I have ever run, and it was simply on the phrase, "You lied to yourselves." I was teaching the group to be in their truth.

Reading Auras and Channeling

I discovered that one of the best techniques to connect with people is to tune in to their aura or energy field, then look back in their lives and see what happened. I try to see when and how it affected them and if it possibly still affects that person's life today.

So many times, before or during a session with a client, because I am channeling, I have no understanding of where my guides – my crowd – are taking me. My crowd will have met up with my client's guides, even if she doesn't know she has got guides. And they will give the facts that are necessary – that are needed – to be able to put the ego actions right.

The lowest form of behaviour, is hurting somebody or punishing somebody, being cruel, being angry, feeling you have the right to abuse somebody... This is what we call *low* ego.

Whereas *Spirit* only has love, compassion, empathy, and joy.

TRUE HEALING COMES FROM LOVE

A Note from Gill: It probably doesn't come as much of a surprise that the final course Denny participated in, the 100-Day Ancient Secrets Experience, was based on a book that begins with this quote:

"I didn't come to teach you.
I came to love you.
Love will teach you."
– *Ancient Secrets of a Master Healer*

Denny lived this quote in her everyday life.

Denny and myself joined with hundreds of people from around the world in the 100-Day course to learn ancient healing secrets behind certain food/nutrition, herbs, home remedies & more. As mentioned earlier, it is through her involvement in this course that the global team of volunteers came together to help make this book a reality.

We'd also join the free online Sunday Global Healing Miracle calls through this, and Denny spoke on one of them, saying that this was the most loving community she'd ever experienced.

Denny understood that deeper healing happens on many levels: mental, emotional, physical, and spiritual… and she was a living ambassador of the teaching that the deepest healing comes from love.

My Life's Work

Getting people back to understanding their love and under-standing their relationship with themselves is my life's work. If they can get that right, their relationship with the world is right. Then they have great value to the world.

It is being able to love who you are and realise you are abso-lutely what you are meant to be. And these fabulous learnings and various wounds and pains and injuries that you have had are intentional by *Spirit*. Not so much to have the pain, but to move beyond the need for it, and to come to love. You see, if you simply are love, nothing can get at you. You are just looking at everything with a smile.

"LOVE is the only truth."

PART TWO

Sessions with Denny

A Note From Gill

Denny worked with people for over forty years. She worked as a hypnotherapist, psychotherapist, healer, psychic, and counsellor, and has seen thousands of people from all over the world. To understand how Den worked, we set up zoom sessions for people who wanted to work with Den and were happy for us to use part of their sessions in the book. Most of the client's names are changed to protect their privacy. Denny wished for these sessions to be included so that they may guide you on your journey and help to raise your vibration.

Denny always repeated messages to emphasise their significance and to gain her clients' attention. If you are noticing certain messages repeating, pay attention; they are flashing up because they might apply to you.

"It took me years and years and years to really understand that the lessons were all to do with me. I couldn't blame all those out there because they were all wonderful players."

"Remember what you are really made of. What all of us are made of. It takes us so many lifetimes – many lifetimes – to gather that we are actually Love."

Session #1: Jo

Rid Yourself of Fear, Anxiety, & Guilt
Using the Golden Circle

Gill: Jo, a mother of three young children, was going through a tough patch and experiencing tremendous amounts of anxiety. Every day she went through huge emotional turmoil and could not think straight. She had to take time off work and couldn't really care for her children.

Denny: What have we come together for today?

Jo: I guess I am not in a good place right now. For the past few weeks, I have been in a state of panic and anxiety, and I am not 100% sure what is going on. I have a few ideas. I have the constant ability to worry about every single thing that goes on in my life. Everything! And I catastrophize everything. I always see the negative in everything. I see the worst outcome possible, and no matter what I have tried to do, so far it doesn't seem to go away.

I just don't know what has happened to me these last few weeks, but I just cannot seem to get out of a state of panic. Or if I do, one minute I seem to be okay and the next minute suddenly my chest is so tight I can't breathe and I feel like I am dying. I feel like I am having some kind of heart attack or something else is going on. I just don't know.

Denny: There are things that are affecting a tremendous amount of us at the moment. The planet's vibration has been gradually rising, but in the last six months, it has speeded up and of course because we are on the planet, we have gone up with it.

Everything that is living has been affected. Scientists measure the planets against each other to see which planet is moving where, and our earth is doing a completely upward trend. This is having a very profound effect on a lot of us, from bringing in depression or a lot of yesterday's stuff, including fears and panics.

But it is also bringing in new stuff, like new growth. But we are having trouble getting our bodies used to it. So, if you are feeling muddled over the last few weeks, I am not remotely surprised, because the vast majority of us are feeling that way. I, for example, keep 'fine checking' myself, asking, *"Where am I? Am I still in my truth? Am I still okay with what is going on?"*

I am not a believer in living in fear. I create my reality. I discovered that if I really got hold of my life, I could change everything and stop giving my power away to my ego, which is my lowest intelligence as a human. If I listened to the truth, which is my *Spirit* – which is what I am, which is what you are – I could make a difference for me. Once I learned that, I had a say in what was going on with my life.

As a child of course, I had no control or say, and I was terrified through all the pain and toture. It was just a nightmare. It took many years to start to be aware that I actually could have a big say in what was going on.

Looking at everything that was going on, the only common denominator from beginning to end was me. Therefore, I was meant to be there. And that is when I started to connect with *Spirit*. My beloved *Spirit* was always saying, *"Yes, this is what it is all about!"* It is coming back to discovering that you are love. That you are the truth and don't answer to your lower self – which is the ego – which is your emotional reaction with fear of this or terror of that.

A lot of our world seems to be based on fear. I am a very stubborn Denny. You can probably tell I have never gone along with the status quo. I have gone along with my truth and how I felt. I won't live in fear because that is not what my life is all about. But I live with millions who do, and it is mucking us *all* up because their energy is hitting ours. If you have got children, it is hitting them without them knowing what it is all about. Your husband?

Jo: My partner, we are not married.

Denny: You have a partner. Okay, well, the same thing would be happening to him. It is because you have been exposed, darling girl, to the rise of the planet and its energies, and you have got nowhere to run and hide, because you can't get back down to the level Earth was.

We have to adjust to the best of our ability, which we can, when we suddenly realise, *"If I said yes to being born while all this is going on, it means I have got a reason for being here. I have got a purpose. God only knows what it is, but I have got my Spirit who wouldn't have sent me back now, unless there was something for me to do."*

None of us come back just random. We come back with a reason. Our job is to try and find that reason before we die, or else we go back and say, *"Oh really? Was that what it was all about? Oh golly... how stupid of me. I should have seen that."* It is that kind of life and you have seen that and in comes another lesson.

Let's go back to your fear. Why are you choosing fear at this moment?

Jo: I am not sure why am I choosing fear. I think I have always lived in fear, even before this pandemic.

Denny: Have you got paper and pencil with you?

Jo: Yes.

Denny: Write down the word *fear*. What other emotions come straight up? What else is coming up that is drowning you at the moment?

Jo: Guilt?

Denny: That is a good one! That is an interesting one, because guilt is one of the emotions that you can only be taught externally, either by your beloved parents or by your teachers at school. By the time you reach seven, eight, or nine, you have already got guilt, but you didn't make it. It was given to you. For example, it could be a parent's point of view that if you don't do *that*, *this* will happen. Or you *haven't done* this or that.

> *Guilt or fear comes from, "I am not good enough or I am not worthy. I am going to be found out for being faulty."*

So, the first question is, "Who is going to find you out? What are they going to find out? And what is so awful about you that if anybody finds out about it you are going to be a nothing?"

Jo: I think I have been, for a long time, not wanting to be in a relationship. I have been trying to work out whether it is me, or whether I don't want to be with him. I don't know.

Denny: How long have you been together?

Jo: We have been together for ten years.

Denny: Ten years. Are you feeling guilty because of that? And if so, why?

Jo: Because I feel like, if my truth is that I am not meant to be in this, then I shouldn't be here. I should leave.

Denny: Why are you feeling guilty about that?

Jo: Because it is not fair to him.

Denny: Excuse me? Whose life are we talking about here? We are not down here to run other people's lives. We are involved in other people's lives, but we each have our own line of life. You are born here, and you travel your line of life until you go home.

Beside you are your siblings, they also come from *Spirit*. All the experiences they are going through have been asked for by *Spirit* coming to them. So, you have got those, and then you have got your partner, and you'll have your parents, and you'll have others. But the main lines that are attached to you are separate lines, and each one is owned by a *Spirit*.

That is terribly important to understand, that everyone is learning. This is a school of life, which is a very accurate way of putting it and very true.

Let's come back to your line. The only one you have to answer to, with 100% honesty and truth, is your line, is your *Spirit*. And it is *not* saying, *"I can't do it, because I will hurt and be upset."*

It is saying, *"I have grown tremendously in ten years. I am a very different person to what I was ten years ago. My partner is not travelling with me, and that is perfectly alright. That is his right. If I am the cause of hurt initially, I am still the gift that he is going to need as part of his journey. I have to follow my truth. It is how I best help him. But I have to be me, to have the life that my Spirit asked of me. I don't want to repeat all this again, but I need to give myself time."*

I have an exercise which I get all my students to do for me when we are in a muddle or don't know what we are doing.

Exercise: The Golden Circle

- Can you imagine a golden circle on the ground in front of you and stand in it?
- I'd like you to see if you can drop every negative thought into that circle.
- Stay there until you feel you have dropped everything that is not necessary into that circle.
- Only when you feel you have dropped everything that is negative, do I want you to climb out of the circle.
- Stop holding on to it! Drop it! Drop it!

Denny: I am watching your energy field. The annoying thing is I can see energy. Drop it. You are using it almost as an excuse, sweetheart. You don't need it. Drop it, and when I chase you, I am coming from a place of love. Drop it. And now you are safe, it is only me. Come on, it is like treacle. Now step out. I want you stepping out of the circle because you are being naughty by not letting go.

- Come on out and just stand there and look. Turn around and look at your circle. Look what you have dropped so far. Also, look at how much you are desperately trying to hold on to, instead of being honest, because you can do what you want with this emotion. At the moment, we are separating, that is all. We are not demanding. There is never a demand. Love cannot demand.

Denny: The only way you can see and feel what is going on with you is by standing outside of the pain and the muddle and the emotional baggage that you are sitting in at the moment. When you are standing on the outside looking, your body is free of it.

- Now what I want you to do is walk a pace back away from the circle, but your eyes are kept on the circle, witnessing that the emotions stay there. They stay there. All the muddles, all the upset, all the *I have had enough of a relationship, it is all too much*, it stays there, not in you. It is there in the circle.
- If you can still feel it, step back another step, and again, watch the circle. Perfectly safe, all the emotional negative sits there and you are observing it without being in it.
- Again, let's take another step and we watch and look at the muddle, and the sad, and the upset and this and that. It is in the circle. It is not in you. It is in the circle.

Denny: How does your body feel?

Jo: I feel more relaxed.

Denny: Can you still feel the pain? If so, then let's take another step back, keeping an eye on all that despair, fear, panic, guilt. Reward yourself ten out of ten for guilt. Now stop and feel yourself again looking at your circle. How do you feel?

Jo: I feel a bit lighter.

Denny: Good! Where do you feel guilt? In your heart? Where would you first learn guilt? Who taught you?

Jo: Probably my parents.

Denny: Where did you, if you can remember, where did you really learn your fear of guilt?

Jo: Hmmm, from my dad. He made us feel very guilty for our behaviour towards my mum. He told us that my mum was very ill, when she wasn't. We only found out years later. So, we were constantly being told off for not helping around the house or for not doing this or not doing that, for arguing and making my mum ill.

Denny: Have you talked to these major guilty people? Has it ever crossed your mind, what a brilliant teacher your dad has been for you?

Jo: He has taught me that I shouldn't believe what people, or everyone tells me.

Denny: Absolutely! Absolutely! You chose him. So why did you choose him? What is this lesson that *Spirit* came down for? You came down for a reason, for a main lesson. There are thousands of lessons, but the main one, which I think you are at and asked to learn about, is your guilt and the fear that is interfering with your life today. It is still childlike if you look at it. It is not a grown-up's fear.

> *It took me years and years and years to really under-stand that the lessons were all to do with me. I couldn't blame all those out there because they were all wonderful players.*

Then I discovered that *I chose* my parents. That was hysterical. I gradually found I couldn't blame. The blame game went out the window because the common denominator in every scene that I was being shown was me. Gradually, I realised that it was me that had to do the changing.

It was me that had to see what I was doing. I was very good at running away. To stand in a place never crossed my mind. I had to be able to *see*. I didn't use any of the other tools that we all have – smell, kinesthetic, or any of them. I didn't. I had to be able to *see* it. If I couldn't see, I was a disaster zone. I grew up with claustrophobia.

One day I met up with a phenomenal teacher who sat me in a chair, got to know me, and put a mask around my eyes. I was hysterical with fear, with panic, absolute panic, and that is all we did for about two months, because I couldn't cope with anymore. I couldn't see and it didn't matter. I knew I was in a chair, and he said, "I don't want to lose this. I want to activate your 'feel' because you are basically a feeler, but you are terrified. You actually live on, "If I can see, I can run for cover. I can protect myself if I can see."

When you have these realisations arriving, your conscious brain goes, *"Hang on a moment, he is quite right. If I can't see, I am an absolute disaster."* It was years later that I learned how to stop being a disaster for different reasons, but he was phenomenal. He activated my kinesthetic, my hugs, my cuddles, everything that I had missed, and so desperately needed, into my life for the very first time. I learned that if I worked at it, I could embrace something if I faced my fear. That became the most important thing. You are not facing Denny, you are running.

Now I can be terrified, but I won't run. I will now stand my ground and my knees no longer shake. I can actually stand my ground, not knowing what I am going to do, but trusting me and trusting that *Spirit* knows perfectly well what is going on and will assist.

So here is your list:

Number one: You have to stop running. You don't have to do anything else at the moment. You can even run if you want to. There is no demand in love. We can only start drawing a road, a map, so that we can get hold of bits of us. Everything you do will be done in love, even though your ego wants you to think absolutely the opposite.

Ego is very low, and it hits all of our painful, really sore emotions. Guilt, anger, fear, jealousy, not good enough. Not good enough is a brilliant one. I think we all carry that one, and if you are able to go, *"I chose my beloved parents."* Brilliant. *"Why did I choose them?"*

We then start to look at, okay, on the mother's side, well both sides, you are going to have the ancestral traffic in your own being, so we put our ancestral traffic aside for the moment.

The next part of our looking is, "Okay, they have had power over me because I was a child." I came to them for my learning – good learning, bad learning, no learning – depending on what your *Spirit* wanted you to have a go at. It sounds like your parents have done a very good job so far. Your mother played "I am ill," and allowed your father to go on playing the game of "she is ill."

Jo: Yes. And he doesn't even know if it is true himself.

Denny: So why did you choose him? Give me a wonderful quality about him.

Jo: When I reflect on the way I have been as a parent: he taught us how to brush our teeth, he taught us all those simple things that I am struggling with as a parent. We were looked after. I think we had everything but emotional support.

Denny: Everything except?

Jo: Yes. So, we had everything that we could need in life, and he taught us how to behave in the world as such and with people.

Denny: Let's get that corrected; he told us his version of –

Jo: Yes, his version.

Denny: Change the statement darling girl. Not your way, *his* way.

Jo: Yes.

Denny: At what stage, if at all, did you kick against his regime?

Jo: Teenager. No, actually before that. I remember when he used to be a bit rough with my brother, and I would be screaming at him, "How dare you do that? How dare you behave like that? How dare you hurt my brother!" I always was really sticking up for my brother. I can remember that from a young age.

I remember rebelling against my dad because we used to have jobs to do around the house, and my jobs were always, in my opinion, the feminine jobs. And I'd say, "Why have I got to do the ironing? Why isn't my brother doing the ironing? Why am I not doing the gardening, and all of that stuff?" I remember rebelling against that when I was probably a teen, teenage years, and really getting angry.

Denny: How is your brother as an adult?

Jo: Well, not in a good place really, because my brother lost his wife a few years ago. I didn't speak to my parents for a long time because my brother's wife died from a brain tumour. Previous to that, my mum told my brother that *she* had a brain tumour, which was a lie. So, he's not in a good place really.

Denny: Oh, bless him and remember that his *Spirit* knows perfectly well what journey he is on. We very rarely find a 'why we are on' or 'those that we love are on.' All we can do is love and support. We cannot run their lives for them. We can only empathise and be compassionate.

∞

Exercise: Imagine Life Is Like A String

- *You start from the one end and follow the string.*
- You are born and you travel all along this lovely line of life, which is not a line.
- It has ups and downs, and bumps and circles, and comes back to yourself, and so on.
- It is a wonderful life you can imagine, and beside you are all the others.
- Now if you put your brother there, you have to be careful that you don't leave your line to go on to his line to protect him.
- Your line is your *Spirit.*
- It is your life and that is the life your beloved Spirit who has asked you to trace, follow, go through the hell of learning.
- We can only love others; we cannot jump over and rescue.
- His *Spirit* will know exactly what is going on.

That is all your brother's pain, sweetheart, not yours. It is your pain for him that is not yours to carry, and yet look at the load. Look at the load, sweetheart, you are carrying. That is not your life. If you were meant to be your brother, you would have been, you wouldn't be Jo. You can love, you can be compassionate, but we cannot own. His *Spirit* knows what he is going through. If he ever connects to his *Spirit*, he will suddenly find the greatest strength he could find, which is of course himself.

Why do you feel you have to carry so much?

Jo: I guess I always did from when we were younger. My brother was ten. I think he was the first person my mom told that she had cancer. My friend was over at the time. My brother came running up the stairs, because I had been waiting for mom to take me and my friend to a party, and he came running up the stairs because I had asked him to go and find out why she was taking so long. He came running up the stairs and screaming at me, "Mom has got cancer!"

It was as if our world was just turned upside-down. I felt I needed to protect him because I was the one that made him go and find out what she was doing. She was obviously in whatever space she was in at that time and decided to blurt it out to him, this little boy! We lived with it for so long. We lived believing it for such a long time, and it felt like I had to protect him. I guess either way I felt like it was up to me because my parents didn't do anything.

Denny: Well, they did, they did – they became the fraud. Sweetheart, it is not yours to carry. I want you to let it out because you never let it go fully. I don't want you going through that again. Go back in that circle back there. You need this out of your system because it is getting in the way of your life. That is not giving you any freedom with your life. It is so in your face.

Jo: Even though I know that it is not true now, it is still so deeply rooted in me because it was part of my being for such a long time. And they still are not admitting it to us, but I know it is not true.

Denny: We will find out why they chose you and your brother. It is a form of cruelty. It is an interesting one. I was doing a case the other day about the closeness between love and hate. The line between love and hate is so close in what we are dealing with, it was really quite frightening.

Leave your tragedy in that circle. We can pull that bit out when we want to have a look at it. It is not pushed away, but we are just not standing in it. We are refusing to allow it into our bodies because it's not our stuff. The feeling is what we are being given to understand. It doesn't actually belong to us.

> *What I learned to do in my orphanage days was to go up with Spirit because I didn't know what else to do. That was the only tool I had. But as years went by and the various pain came in, and the learning came in, and life went on, I discovered that there was so much more out there if I would stand still and have a look at it, instead of running.*
>
> *From there it built until I got to a stage where I could then go, "I don't need that emotion, I am going to put it over there. I need to see it, but I don't want to push it away, because I haven't dealt with it, so it will come back and bite me on the nose at some stage. I need it there for when I am ready to look at it." That is how I progressed bit by bit.*
>
> *Through it I discovered that there is only one answer in everything we do, and that is love.*
>
> *We are the ones that demote love. We are the ones that go, "Yes, but I want to get out of this relationship. I want this, I want that, and it makes me a bad person." When did Spirit say that? It hasn't, has it? No, it is human. It is like saying, "Well that is daft, because that is not what I am supposed to do with my life – live a lie." It is understanding when I say you are number one, there is not an ego energy anywhere.*

You are number one because your number one is your Spirit. That is what you really are. You are not a human having a human experience or having a Spiritual experience. You are a Spirit, having a human experience.

Denny: *Spirit* set the whole thing up, which I think is very unfair. Being psychic the way I am, I was able to go back up and float around out of my body a lot. When I went back to have a look as to why I chose the life I chose, of course the one thing I forgot was that if there is no human involved, there is no ego. So, I sailed up and it was just a wonderful love field, and I was shown my life as a linear life, not a *Spirit's* life which is continuous all the time now.

Which is why as far as your brother is concerned, you also have a past life issue. You do know that, don't you? You have a past life issue there, which is why you are so close. That is why it is so strong in this one. Now the first thing we see straightaway: this is *past* life, as well as *this* life, but it is interfering with this life. Can you recognise that? You are gradually understanding that the love you have for your brother has slumped everything in your life.

We can't really sort this life out until we have eased that relationship with your brother. So, we need to be able to say to him, or to yourself, "I love you very, very much but I am letting you go. I am letting you be all that you are, and I support you, and comfort you from here. But I am not your life."

Jo: It's so painful! Very painful.

Denny: I am aware! It is the number one love. It is on top of your family, it is on top of everything. Would you say that this is what you want? That this is what *Spirit* would have you do?

Jo: Yes.

Denny: So Spirit would like you to love your brother more than your family?

Jo: Oh sorry, no!

Denny: No! Do you know what *Spirit* is asking of you? What do you think your beloved *Spirit* is asking of you?

Jo: Love? I don't know.

Denny: What is your *Spirit* asking you to look at? Why does your brother own all your love and your other loves are secondary?

Jo: I don't know.

Denny: Do you think your *Spirit* is happy that your love for your brother is greater than that for your children? Your partner? Your parents and whoever else?

Jo: No.

Denny: Why not?

Jo: Because he is not. He is not the only person in my life.

Denny: Well, number one, we can't run somebody else's life. We can only run our own. This is where compassion and empathy come in. But you sweetheart, you are sitting a lot on *his* line of life and not on *yours* and it is completely defeating your ability to love others in the way that your being would be looking at love.

I think when I look back now, I am being shown that you have parented your brother unsuccessfully two times. I think you were his mother many lifetimes ago, and that is probably why you have such a strong attachment.

I am definitely aware that you are the mother of him, and I am aware that he doesn't live very long, and the blame game starts there. I have got four or five lifetimes since then, with nothing to do with that at all. In fact, in this life you start breaking that connection.

He needs his freedom too, he needs his freedom from you, as much as you need the freedom from him.

You can go back on the right track, so your decisions that are going on now will be the correct ones.

Jo: I barely ever know what the right decision is in anything.

Denny: Don't make any decisions at all at the moment because you are not anywhere near where you need to be. I would like you to please, with great love, do some homework and please look at your relationship with your brother, and look at your relationship with your parents. All is done with great love, but you still put the truth down.

Unfair-bully-cruel-you put down the absolute truth that is in you in relationships with both. Next time, we are going to hand back two-thirds of those parcels to your parents. Start off-loading their behaviour towards their son that you are carrying, so that you are freed up there. We then have more space, with love between what's really going on and their lies. Fascinating you chose them. Fascinating they are the teachers. I don't want you to do anything else except understand that you are number one and your *Spirit* is waiting for you to check in.

> *Remember what you are really made of. What all of us are made of. It takes us so many lifetimes – many lifetimes – to gather that we are actually Love.*

I don't know how many lifetimes I have been trying to find it. The fact I found it in this lifetime is magic, absolute magic. I shudder to think what the next place will be like, with another one waiting around the corner, but it is so rewarding. It is so beautiful when we really understand that at the end of the day this is all it is that we are dealing with, without any of the ego rubbish emotions.

Please, move gently with you, please. Be more loving towards you. Own your right to have these emotions. Get rid of feeling guilty, it is a waste of time. It's not yours. You have got every right to feel all these emotions. It is how you lovingly work them, sweetheart.

Jo: Okay. Thank you!

Denny: Love you lots. Take care. Lots of Love.

"You are the subject. You are the Spirit. You are down here on behalf of you. Nobody else, nothing else."

Session #2: George

Rescuing Yourself from the Past through Compassion & Letting Go of Shame, Guilt, and Punishment

Gill: George had been going through a lot of emotional pain over the last few years. Additionally, he had been experiencing physical pain to such an extent that he could not work, walk up a hill, or complete simple day-to-day tasks.

Denny: What do you think brought us together today?

George: Well, sorry, I might cry, I'm emotional already.

Denny: We can get as emotional as we want, and that is alright, and it is a lovely way of letting go. It is something I had to learn to do. I am very good at it now.

George: I'm sort of stuck in life and I am on a path of learning and healing, but I have got to this point where I realise I have had some trauma in my past that I think I never saw before. I have been working with a healer. She told me I need to try to have self-compassion and I have realised that it is hard for me to even understand what that is. I have been living at a baseline of self-shame for so long without realising that this is what my life has been and trying to break through has been a challenge.

Denny: It is a lifetime challenge and I think you are doing brilliantly. Looking at your energy field, you have got some lovely colour and some interesting patches of stuck energy... probably with having quite a bit of physical pain, because the energy is banging against your physical body. But there are some beautiful shades there of real worth, of value. I am not too sure if you understand what you are doing down on Earth.

George: Not right now, I don't.

Denny: The first step is to separate us today from us yesterday, emotionally.

George: Yes, I can see how that would be. In the books that I have read about this trauma, they talk about visualising the little child that had the trauma and creating a safe space in your heart for them to be comforted or to love them or hold them.

Denny: It is really the other way around. It is not what we want; it is what do *they* want that we can give them? Your healer was talking about you needing more compassion, was that it?

George: Yes.

Denny: Yes, but towards yourself and an appreciation towards your inner children, of what they went through for you. Because we need to understand that we are the whole project – not what we do, not what we achieve – we are the project. And *Spirit* is watching every move and knows exactly what he put us into.

That is where compassion and empathy come in. We are so good at blaming ourselves through our lack of self-worth. *"I'm not good enough. I don't deserve, or do deserve, punishment."*

George: That is exactly what I have done.

Denny: How can you be compassionate if you are full of the blame game? *"I am the bad one. I deserve all this."* No! The real you is completely as whole and as fantastic as he was when he was born. His journey has become filled up with ego, which is the physical body, and the brain, which feels everything, it unfortunately believes.

When I first discovered that I could actually go back in time into the orphanage and rescue one of my children – one part of me – I had to learn to own that child. I didn't want to know or even own her as part of me. I had to learn to say, "I – me, the child." It was always *'the child'* which I found very interesting for a long time.

The first time I went in, I went with what I thought were good intentions of, *"I know it all. Now, I must go in love and make her better."* But she ran. She ran as fast as she could from me, and I am going after her, *"Hello, it is me! I love you and I am your future. I have come to love you, to thank you, to rescue you to whatever it is you would like."* But all she did was run away.

This child wasn't going to stop. She was going to go on running every time I moved towards her. I stopped eventually. She just fell on the floor in exhaustion because I had the realisation this child had never met anybody going towards her safely with love, with affection, and with care. That is why I was a threat, a major threat.

I then understood the best thing to do was to sit there and do nothing. When she was ready to see if we could make friends, it was purely on her terms, not mine.

Have you shown compassion towards them? Have you thanked them? Have you said, *"Oh my God, look what you went through, look what you have done for me?"*

George: How did you get to the point where you could see that little child? That is the thing. I still don't see the trauma. It is still blocked somehow. Like, I see the wind. I can feel it. I can see the effects on the trees and things.

Denny: Yes. Now this could be your main learning on the list that *Spirit* put down for you to look at. See if you really feel the need of self-shame. These could be your big learning curves. They sound powerful, and I do actually think one of those past lives you have brought through, and the way you are talking about it, is too familiar for this lifetime only.

It is like punishment comes through, but the punishment is you punishing you. It is maybe about time we were able to stop and go, *"So why do I so enjoy punishing myself? What am I really hiding?"*

George: That is a tough one, isn't it?

Denny: We have very good defence mechanisms and you have got a very good one there. *"I am not good. I am useless,"* and more like that. *"Therefore, there is no way I can look at the actual real leader because I am already condemned, therefore unsafe."*

George: That is the one thing I was talking to Dr. Clint about last week, and he gave me a quote: "Only when you are defenceless can you find true safety." I realised that. Like with my wife – we are separated – she hasn't treated me kindly, and I realised that.

Denny: Say that, again, she treated you –

George: Unkindly, to say the least.

Denny: Let's change the statement. I have *allowed* her to treat me unkindly.

George: I realise now that I have enabled her to treat me this way, and that is a realisation that hit home.

Denny: Always say to yourself, *"The quicker we can let what we think about them go, the quicker it will stop."*

She is in the game. She is there because *Spirit* put her there. She is undoing an old pattern that you witnessed through a youngster. It is called trauma, which made you make the very firm statement, *"I'll never do this. Because this is what I have witnessed."*

We choose our beloved parents. We often wonder why, but we choose them for their good and their bad. They are simply humans like us.

∞

Exercise: Parcels

In this wonderfully simple exercise, parents are energetically invited into a special place.

- They either come in gradually, or they come nicely, or they might come in argumentatively, or one of them doesn't come at all. Again, you have no control, but you are calling on the truth of them, as opposed to the ego of them.
- You have in front of you a pile of parcels and each parcel is named.
- One parcel was loaned to you by your parents. It is actually theirs.
- You hand it back to them.
- You say, *"Thank you so much for the loan. I have learned everything I needed to learn. I no longer need it. I return it to you with thanks."*
- You hand it over and either the parent takes it nicely, understandingly, or tries hard to pretend it is not there at all.

What we are doing is realising that the parcels have never been ours. They have been taught to us. Our ego owns them, believing this is who you are. *"I am not good enough. I am bad,"* or *"I am guilty of something terrible."* That is not you. That is the parcels. We don't know who brought them in.

George: So, it is time to learn to give those away.

Denny: Yes! And we have got beautiful exercises to do that. We can shift so much of this, but we need to start with an understanding from you.

You are the subject. You are the Spirit. You are down
here on behalf of you. Nobody else, nothing else. It
doesn't matter how wonderfully healed you become.
It doesn't matter how magnificent the world thinks
you are. That is totally irrelevant as far as Spirit is
concerned because it is only ego that wants to say,
"Oh yes, the world loves me."

A good leader needs a good team. A good leader needs themselves. They will be followed. But they are not looking to be followed. They follow themselves, and it is all inward. They are not looking out for approval. They are not looking out for being pulled to pieces. They are not looking after themselves at all because all they are doing is meeting themselves.

We are all from the same source. We have come back on behalf of our *Spirits* to do our best to go through the learning process. 'School of Life,' it is called. It has got beautiful parts in it, but we have very painful parts, and when we have been truly damaged, it takes a lot of strength, a lot of empathy to self.

It is only when we start to pay attention to the dam-
age to ourselves, that we start to understand what
empathy and compassion really are. We think we can
offer it to others brilliantly. No, we can't.

I am fairly visual, and I have a special place where I would go when I first started to collect my inner children. It was nature. They had little bushes and trees, and somewhere along the line they just knew they were safe. There is a stream, little hills, and a massive great ancient oak tree. When I used to go to meet them as I gathered them, they all came flying towards me. They needed me. They needed my love. They needed proof that I accepted them, what they were.

When I go to check on them now, I might get a wave. They hardly need me at all, and I don't need them because we are no longer separate. I embrace them; they are me. They went through all this for me and my journey. That is when you can offer compassion and Love. That is what Love really is. There is no judgement. There is nothing other than an acceptance of what we are going through, and what we have gone through, and how well we are handling it.

Final thought: Work on yourself – on loving yourself – on accepting your journey.

"To help the world, you have to know you are good enough and accept how much learning you still have to do. Know that you are going to be learning until the day you die."

"Once you understand what Love really is, your life becomes beautiful, opening you up to happiness, fun, and for me, a lot of humour!"

Session #3: Annabelle

Trust Your Truth and
Ask Your Body

Gill: One of Denny's ways to connect with people was to tune in to their aura, or energy field. She would look back in their lives, and see what happened and when, and how it affected them and possibly still affects them today. Annabelle had two sessions with Denny. During the first, Denny could see a couple of time frames that affect Annabelle's life now.

Denny: Hello! Let me tune in to your energies. Your ages are six and 38 to 39 years. Those two areas are affecting your life today. There is so much going on that is still being carried by you.

Annabelle: That is what I don't know or understand. The 38-year-old, I am guessing is when I started trying to get pregnant for my son, which was fairly easy. But the six-year-old, I am not quite sure.

Denny: It's connected to school. Interestingly, it is a male teacher, not a female teacher. I don't think it is the classroom teacher. I am just being shown this sweet little girl – you weren't very big – standing like a statue of fear. There is not much action around you, but I think you believe it is *at* you and you can't handle it.

You are too sensitive. You are too nervous, and you are very frightened of the wolf coming for you. So, you do a cover-up. You start a game of cover-up, where you decide you are not good enough, but nobody else must know. And that has just shattered right through your life. *"I am not really good enough."* Although your common sense knows perfectly well that is rubbish. But your inner being, when the crunch really comes, you back off.

So, for today it would be good to look back at your six-year-old and say to her, *"Hey! You are absolutely brilliant! I am here. Turn around and face me, you'll be perfectly alright."* If she can hear that from you, and feel your strength from her future, she will start to relax. She needs to relax better; she is very stressed and tense.

The picture I am getting so strongly is that the stress and tension is staying within her, and it is still here today. It is part of that overall lack of you bouncing out into freedom. You are so close, but you haven't quite gotten there yet.

You have understood and love yourself, which is lovely to see, but you don't put it into practice as well as you could. We still have others in front of you, instead of realising that *you* are the main subject. You were sent back by *Spirit* into the human form to have this experience of what it is like being *Spirit* trapped inside a body. So many people have it the wrong way around.

They think they are human having a Spiritual experience. No, it is the other way around. We are *Spirit*, having a human experience. It is *Spirit* that has sent us back with our learnings. So, we think we control everything. We don't.

We are steered very lovingly by *Spirit* and by the ego. They work hand in hand. Ego can be a nightmare, but it doesn't mean to upset. It doesn't mean to cause trouble. But when it causes a problem, like it has at age six, the problem stays as a six-year-old. It doesn't develop. Therefore, you can be 20, 69, 12, whatever age you want to be, and you are still going to react as a six-year-old in each given situation where that chord of fear comes in. And that is where the ego starts to get into difficulty.

The other beloved use of ego is to put all the negatives into all our emotional nightmares. But *Spirit* sets it up because we are not down here by accident. We are down here for a special reason, and we couldn't have chosen a more interesting time to be on the planet. Particularly America – so many ups and downs. It is fascinating watching. It is brilliant how America is pulling itself up.

You were well protected, you are still. I am being shown by my crowd, my guides, that love is a problem. Not in the emotion of giving – you have a tremendous amount of love to offer. Where you hold back is the part of you that can't let go. That is one part that I would agree with. You know we cannot give ourselves away, or when we do, we get very badly damaged. We cannot give ourselves away because we are love, we are complete. You hear this awful phrase, 'My other half,' which doesn't belong, which is nonexistent. You can share, but you are actually complete.

Annabelle: Yes, I believe that.

Denny: Yes. You do not need ownership. You do not need looking after, which I love to see. *"I am able to cook with myself. I can share and I can love."* But we have a slight thing on the physical level. I think it is on the physical level of tiredness. I am just following pictures. Can you go back to age nineteen?

Annabelle: At age nineteen, a year after high school, I was not doing anything because I didn't know what I wanted to do. Then my sister sat me on our bed and said, "Choose something."

She made me go through the college courses. So, I chose interior design and architecture and went into that.

I didn't complete it because I got married and didn't continue. I think that was about the age of nineteen.

Denny: Did you give anything up that mattered?

Annabelle: I don't know.

Denny: Go back and feel.

Annabelle: I guess, maybe I gave something up when she sat me down and made me decide something. That wasn't the route that I was choosing. I had to give in to what was normal, and that was that we all went to college. I wanted to be a wild child, but that wasn't allowed.

Denny: How much older is your sister?

Annabelle: She is quite a few years older but less experienced, I would say, because she always lived a more sheltered life.

Denny: So where is your exuberant wild *Spirit*?

Annabelle: Coming out now, I guess. I don't know if she is ever going to come back. Why do I need it again?

Denny: That is why I am asking what is missing.

Annabelle: I guess my more-free self is missing. I was married at a young age for less than five years. It was annulled because he wasn't faithful, and he hid money from me. The unfaithfulness I could handle, but not that he hid money, because I wanted to make money. I wanted to buy and sell houses, but he didn't want me to do it. In the end I just walked away from the marriage because I figured that he wanted control.

The day that I came down the steps from the court to file for divorce was the same day I met my future husband that I have had for the past 30 years. It took us a while to get married because I'd just got out of a relationship and didn't know what I wanted. Then finally after nearly a decade, we got married. And then nearly eight years later we had a baby. I was outgoing and out dancing every night, but I changed for my husband, who I knew was good for me. And then, because my son was not well, I was less social. I needed to be with my son at the time, who is all grown up now.

Denny: Looking at your life, could we say that your life has been one with a lot of suppression?

Annabelle: Yes, I guess.

Denny: The one thing that you wanted is freedom. What do you think *Spirit* sent you back to learn?

When we come back, Spirit has all sorts of agendas for us, but there is always one that is usually the very first one. Or it is one that has been going on for many lifetimes. It is a big one. It is the biggest one in this particular incarnation, and it is now learning at long last that I am basically love.

I can't give myself away because I am complete. I belong to Spirit. I am a Spirit. I am only human this very short period of time trying hard to learn the lessons that Spirit is putting in my path.

I am trying to get an idea of what the main thing is, and when I look at you, it is *suppression*. It is not being allowed the freedom that you have mentally thought you wanted. Or your ego has said, *"You want freedom!"* and your *Spirit* has put situations and scenarios in, time and time again, to make sure you don't.

Annabelle: I think I was put here to help and work with people with disabilities. And instead of going wild and wrong, I can go wild and good. And go full force helping people and give my love this way because I know how to give.

Denny: Yes, you must correct that statement because as far as *Spirit* is concerned, we can't do wrong. We can't do right. There is only learning with every single action. Only the blame game and reduction games are made by us at our lowest intelligence, which is ego.

Everyone is born with an ego. It is human, with a thought pattern. It desperately tries to protect us. It wants to care for us and, as little ones, we end up thinking it is the boss because when one gets angry the ego's made the anger. If ego finds or senses when we are unhappy about something, ego will do all it can to stop that unhappiness from coming back to us. But ego can get stuck in that pattern.

I am looking at you, I think, as a six-year-old, and she is still doing it. Ego can't put that right. Only *Spirit* can. It was a very good move. It was a protection of you. The ego gets in the way because it is made up of all the negative emotions: unfair, false, jealousy, anger, rage, depression, you name it. They all belong to ego. That is ego.

All of our egos are made up of the experiences that we are put into. Your *Spirit* would have already done the map and knows exactly what is happening. *Spirit* knows who the players are, and on some occasions, the players very definitely overstep the mark. Some players don't come up to where they are meant to. But when I do past life work, I have to get permission from *Spirit*, and the others involved in the scene, for a behaviour to change an outcome. Because *Spirit's* lifetime is always that way.

> We are linear. Spirit is now, always, past, present, and future at the same time. If you get permission, you are able to change the life that was then.

Let me give you an example:

One of my clients many years ago came to me with asthma, and we went back into her past life because the answer was there. She was in a past lifetime a male captain on a ship. Not a nice one. Very bossy. Very cruel to the crew and the crew went against him, caught him, and he was strapped to a wooden plank and thrown overboard where he slowly died.

When we came out of that vision, I asked *Spirit* if she had permission to go and change that outcome because it would mean all those that were involved in the murder – my client herself – and any other players around would be affected.

If she were allowed, it would only change if she fully understood why it happened in the first place. No blame game. As the captain, if *he* was able to own the fact that he was an absolute nasty piece of work and he asked for what he got, then *she* would be able to own the fact.

We went back to the ship. They were all on board. There was tranquility. He transformed into a much nicer captain there and then, and by saving that life, all the people involved became who they really were meant to be, and now they aren't carrying that weight.

When she came out of the experience for a second time, she was free of that nightmare. She didn't have asthma anymore. The asthma was because she couldn't breathe in the previous lifetime. Now her lungs worked perfectly because she didn't have that experience anymore!

Denny: Somebody once asked me, "Why don't you go back and find out why you came back this time around? What did you come back to really learn this time?"

I went back to my crowd, and of course completely forgot the physical – my ego – wouldn't be there. I was pure essence. I was pure *Spirit* and *Spirit* showed me my life that I chose *this* time. One part was black, and the rest looked lovely and from love. I said, *"Oh yes, I can handle that,"* because of course there is no ego. So, to say, "I really don't want *that* life, I'd like to choose a *different* one," would have been coming from an ego place.

Your ego is your physical, and it carries all the pains and the wounds physically, mentally, and emotionally. We are working our way through all this to come back to the truth – that we are simply Love. If we really understand what Love is, nothing can touch us. It is a level of trust.

Here is another very good example:

I had a client many years ago, a young woman. She worked with me for about two years and became very spiritually aware.

She had no job and suddenly she got a note saying there was a job offer. It was for a personal assistant, included a car, and everything she wanted – sensible salary and everything else. She had learned never to ask ego, but to ask truth, which is *Spirit*. It is a feeling. It is not the head. It is a feeling.

I teach different ways where you can test through asking your body. One of them is the pendulum response, where your body responds by moving forward and backward. There is nothing that your *Spirit* doesn't know. It is miles ahead of you in knowledge from where we are today or yesterday.

So, she felt into it. She had been offered the job, fantastic, but her *Spirit* said, *"No."*

She couldn't believe it. She said, *"I am terribly sorry, Spirit, I have made a mistake, obviously, but I have just been offered this lovely job. I am just checking with you that it is okay to do it,* and back again came the word, *"No."* It took tremendous courage. Tremendous courage on her part to turn the job down.

Her family turned against her. How dare she say no to a job! Every negative ego thought was thrown at her. She had, herself, questioned her own ability.

I said, "You can only trust. Do you trust or do you not trust? That is the answer. Do you trust what you are feeling?"

"Yes," she said, "but painfully."

Three weeks later, she got another note, and it was for another PA job with a car and so on – almost identical to the one she turned down. After the interview, she got offered the job and went to *Spirit* and said, *"Please, Spirit, is this okay to start this job?"* Back came *"Yes!"* So, with great relief, she took the job.

Six months later, the first firm that offered her a job went bankrupt, so she would have been out of a job! *Spirit* knew all about that. Her ego didn't know anything about it. She trusted what her *Spirit* was saying and was proven right. That is a level of trust that so many of us haven't got but which we can all learn.

> *If you are in an emotion that has got the quality of too much emotion, you cannot be in your truth, because truth hasn't got an emotion to it other than truth. It doesn't have despair, or anger, it doesn't have anything. It is simply a truth.*

If *Yes* is the answer or *No* is the answer, the body simply tells you. But our ego will produce every emotion as to why you *have to* do the opposite of what you thought – doing the opposite of what *Spirit* has said.

Spirit doesn't judge. *We* do the judging, human ego. We are taught to compare ourselves to others from a very small age. *"Am I better? Am I worse? Am I prettier? Am I uglier? How am I in comparison?"* When it should be, *"I am just wonderful. I am just absolutely who I am meant to be. I am on my journey, and it is exciting and yes, it is possibly going to have some hurts along the way. But it's not going to make me faulty or not good enough, unless I let ego in and think it."*

> *To help the world, you have to know you are good enough and accept how much learning you still have to do. Know that you are going to be learning until the day you die.*

I said to my daughter the other day, my last dying words are going to be, "Oh God, it was as simple as that!"

The journey never stops, but it is done in such love. It is such an honour to the *Spirit* that you really are. You are not an ego. You are living in an ego body – the body and the lowest *Spirit*.

The lower ego is where all learning comes from, but *Spirit* put it there and it is learning to talk very early.

If you really look at how brilliant man is at finding fault with love, finding fault with self – we are so good at it – and yet Love is what we are. When you realise that is what *Spirit* is, and it is asking us to come through these wounded souls without blame game, and with an understanding of why we chose to have this experience, and understand the players involved, you have blame game without anything to blame. Knowing that the players, like our parents, came on the stage because we asked them to be part of our learning, which is when we start to take responsibility.

When I went to look at my life to ask, "Why did I choose this life?" There was a section of black, the rest was all blissful. What I hadn't realised, was that the black part could be so damaging and could possibly take a lifetime putting it right. I might go under with it, or I might become this wonderful person that has discovered what love is and take responsibility for everything.

Nobody is at fault. They played a part, and from it all I have discovered that if an ego emotion is there, it cannot be *Spirit*, because *Spirit* won't have that emotion.

If you are really angry about something, you are in ego. You don't take action, you don't do anything, you leave it alone and you put it on the back burner. Try saying, *"I can see you, but I am not dealing with you now."*

You come back and you wait. You will not go to that back burner until you can go to it completely calm and settled and say, *"I can take full responsibility for this. I will look at it now."*

You might have to look for a while and really let it go again, but don't take an action. You don't do anything until you get the full understanding of what it is all about. You can take as long as it wants. It is so gentle. It is the gentleness that is so important, and the more you understand what love of self is all about, the more value you are in the world. You are showing the world what love really is and how to be the True Love, not pretend love.

∞

Exercise: The Golden Circle

As a starter point, if you have got an emotion, then it isn't going to be the truth. Wait until the emotion has gone, then put it to one side.

- Put a golden circle in front of you on the floor, then go and stand inside the circle and drop all the negative thoughts, just drop them into the circle.
- The circle is golden because gold is love and you just stand there and drop, standing there until everything is dropped.
- When you think you have got rid of as much as you can, step out, but keep watching your circle containing what you have dropped, and gradually step away, followed by another step away and another.
- How does the body feel having left all the negative stuff you were covered in, back in the circle?
- The usual response from my clients is they feel better the further back they go, even though they can see it, knowing they can go to it when they want to, as they are the ones in control now.
- They are no longer in the emotion which is made up of ego. This is not blaming ego. There is no blame game anywhere. These are all lessons and learnings.

Watch your language relating to you. Take no action that is not respectful to you and all that you are. No action. Honour who you are and let *Spirit* know you love your *Spirit*. *"I am aware you have set the whole of this up. I love and honour you and I am going to learn to live my life through you, not through ego."* Every time you find yourself getting emotional, put it in the Golden Circle, in the knowledge this is an ego response. You know it's there and can face and deal with it when you are ready.

Coming from a place of love and all the positives that fill your life, you discover you haven't got room or time for any of the other emotions, they are just not there. You start to handle situations in a different way. If somebody comes at you in an angry way, you offer no feelings. It may be you let them get it off their chest, or you remove yourself. Instead of getting angry or saying something in anger, just give and offer love.

> *I have a wonderful group of guides who have been with me from birth. When I was being seriously abused, I was taken out of my body to be with them and kept safe. Of course, I have physical problems today because the body is facing the consequences from the abuse. That is okay.*
>
> *Once you understand what love really is, your life becomes beautiful, opening you up to happiness, fun, and for me, a lot of humour!*

*"It is Love and that is the greatest thing
I have learned!"*

Session #4: Sharmini

Here & Now
Ego, Emotions, Perfection,
Self-Love, and Essence

Denny: You have some beautiful lines in your aura that I can see, some beautiful colours. You have got some patches which you carry on your right shoulder area that are from wounds of an emotional kind. They seem to have damaged the body, but your colours are lovely. There is a steady build-up of colour the more you believe in yourself. But we have got quite a way to go to where you actually believe your worth.

I don't think you have understood yet that you are actually the project. You are the being that *Spirit* sent back to play this role that *Spirit* chose for you.

We didn't choose. We came back because *Spirit* wanted more learning before we came back into a body. Therefore, we cannot feel the ego, which is our human body. So, we can't feel what anger is, what pain or cruelty is. We can't feel it unless we are in it physically.

Our beloved bodies go through so much learning on our behalf. One of the biggest things we could be much better at is being able to acknowledge those ages of us that went through really difficult passages. I didn't, at first. It is a bit like we forget that the woman today didn't experience any of those pains. We carry the ages of those of us that experienced it. So, because of that we are not very good at healing those parts of us that have done so much work for us.

117

Sharmini: It has been a journey for the last year, and I still do not like or love myself that much.

Denny: Why?

Sharmini: I don't know. I just don't love myself.

Denny: Does that mean that you are not loving your *Spirit*?

Sharmini: Yes, because sometimes when I do meditation, I just get a block and think, *"What is wrong? What's wrong?"* I keep asking myself. I don't know.

I am looking after my mum. She is over ninety and a very strong woman but has had dementia these last five years.

Denny: Difficult. Very difficult.

Sharmini: It is progressing quite badly, so she shouts a lot. I don't want to give her all these strong medications that make her a zombie. I just don't want to do that because I want her to be a little bit of her old self. It comes up once in a while, but it is a hard time for me.

Denny: That is very, very hard.

Sharmini: I suppose I am taking some of that in me, most probably.

Denny: Yes, yes. If we look at the ego emotions, which is what we are all brought up on, every emotion is negative, which is why you can always tell the difference.

You are telling the truth, which I call *Spirit*. When you are telling the truth everything is smooth. It doesn't matter how wobbly you are or how upset or anything like that, your body knows the truth. It knows, and when we are not in our truth — when ego joins in — we have an uncomfortable part of us.

Where I think some confusion is coming in is that your ego has every right to let off steam with Mum, because it is the ego that is going through the actions of looking after her. To blame yourself and feel angry that you shouldn't be feeling like that, I think, is very unfair and very unkind to your beautiful being that has said it will do this.

Sharmini: I do tell myself, *"I am love. My mum is love."* Then it is good for a few hours. But then it tilts and turns around, because she gets very physical and she gets very angry, or something like that. I have tried to tell myself, *"I love my mum, everybody is love."*

Denny: In real life we can love people but we will move away from them. In my growth and development over the years, I have had friends that I have gradually lost because they weren't able to understand where I had started to come from, and I wasn't able to stay with where they were coming from, which is purely ego life.

The friendships, the love has been there, but we parted. We distanced ourselves from how we used to be because we were no longer compatible. But we are still just as lovely, though my path took me this way and their path took them that way. They were not compatible, but it doesn't make them anything other than love. I could not stay with them or be with them for any length of time without my whole inner being going, *"I can't cope."* I'm sure when your beloved mother, in her magical age, is loud and shouting, it must be extraordinarily tiring.

Sharmini: Oh, yes. It is tiring!

Denny: Yes, it is you who gets tired, so it is important for that part of you to hear you say *"You are doing brilliantly,"* and love who you are. Everything was chosen by your *Spirit* for you to return to do the learning that your *Spirit* wanted you to do. So, everything about you is perfect.

Sharmini: Yes. I read the book, *The Soul Plan,* and so I accept the journey that I have taken.

Denny: Yes, but you don't accept you.

Sharmini: Yes, that is right. It is an ongoing process, I suppose, because I am doing and studying a lot of things. I have done a lot of other stuff about Spirituality, to gain my *Spiritual* strength from there so that it will help me. That is what I have done the last year. I have been doing just that.

Denny: Congratulate yourself. Number One! Say, *"Well done, me! Well done! I have got this far, and I am finding my way."*

What I don't think you fully understand yet – and it took me, and so many of my students, years and years to understand – is that *we are the project.* Not what we do or what we can achieve. Not that *"I am psychic,"* or *"I can do this or I can do that."* That has got nothing to do with the Denny that is sitting here.

This is the ego Denny sitting in this human form being steered by a wonderful *Spirit.* So, I talk about "we" all the time because it certainly isn't me on my own, but *we.* I love the me who is sitting here. I can't walk very well, my hands don't work very well, but it is me. And what it has been through in this life,

I didn't go through any of it. I carry all the ages that did, and I love them.

When I first met these little girls, which were *me*, I wouldn't even call them *me*. I wouldn't own them. It took a long time to realise that ego had made an assumption that this little girl had to be horrible and nasty to have that kind of thing done to her. *"She was dirty. She was this. She was that."*

What had she done wrong? She had all the blame thrown at her from a future me, and it was learning that, which was a lesson from *Spirit*.

Every step I take, *Spirit* is there with me. When *Spirit* finds that we are not loving it and yet we are doing absolutely what is asked of us, then *Spirit* goes, *"I can only sit here and wait for you to understand that the love you are trying to give everybody else – you can't, until you can give it to yourself."*

You have to feel that ownership that your *Spirit* has. It has nothing to do with ego. Ego is not in on this. This is the sheer truth of you and the beauty of you. You came in beautifully. You are beautiful, but so full of the journey's wounds and the bruises. But you are still absolutely what *Spirit* had asked you to be.

Sharmini: My future journey, which is why I wanted to take this course towards holistic healing, is I want to heal people. That is why I am learning a lot of different modalities to help me on this journey as well, which I hope to achieve in five years' time.

Denny: You will! You will! But you must start by healing yourself.

Sharmini: Yes, I know, that is where it starts.

Denny: We call it, "Clean your own backyard," before you try to help somebody else. It is the gradual understanding of how much we are overrun by our ego from our experiences. How many habits we have. And mostly, how many opinions we have that are ingrained from parents, grandparents, from society. We have no idea that we are so far off the correct mark.

Sharmini: Yes! Let me mention judgement. I am always in judgement of people. Of myself. I took a course which says that judgement is all we learn from outside. You don't come to the world with judgement. It is what you pick up from your parents, the society, and we have to learn to let go of that judgement.

Denny: *Spirit* doesn't have any of these words. They are all ego words. *Spirit* knows one word and that is *learning*. Be it good, be it well done, be it bad, be it horrific, be it whatever the ego thinks – *Spirit* calls it learning, end of story. That is all it is, and we are finding our way through the learnings that our *Spirit* wants us to explore.

Let me share an example:

I talk a lot with my students about overseeing a river. There is water, and stones are sticking up, and we are sailing along quite happily until we hit a rock. We go on hitting the same rock and it doesn't matter what we are trying to do, we don't seem to be able to get past the rock.

Eventually something inside us goes, *"Maybe if I do this differently it might help,"* and suddenly we do a jump, a growth, and we go sailing past the rock. We are back in free-flowing water, just floating blissfully, warmly along. We do that for a while and *Spirit* goes, *"Well done, well done!"* and now we are ready for the next hurdle.

This is when ego gets in the way because ego goes, *"I am not good enough, nobody else is having such difficulties as me."*

And yet every single one of us is the same. I am back doing my journey and learning. You are back. We come from the same source, but we forget. Your learning – you do it on behalf of so many of us in the world. My learning – I do it on behalf of the world and because we come from the same source.

Learning starts with:
- I love who I am.
- I love the *Spirit* that I am.
- I thank *Spirit* for giving me everything I have got and the lessons I am learning, and I am very willing to carry on learning.
- I condemn and judge nothing because it is a learning here.
- It can be a painful one, it can be a lovely one, but I am not going to judge it.
- I am living in love.
- That is all it can be.

It doesn't have any of the ego emotions left. There is no anger, there is no hate, there is no judgement, there is no blame game, there is no depression, there is no nothing. It is just love.

So, if somebody comes towards me, very rude or very unhelpful, I will be 'in love' at them and they will ultimately get really uncomfortable, because they know that they are not in their truth. I am very comfortable, but I am still in love. I will not argue, I will leave. But they will be the ones that feel uncomfortable because they were not in their truth. I know perfectly well that I will find it when I am ready, when it is meant to be found. There is no intensity in what I do because the time will be right when it is right.

You are wanting to do all these things – beautiful, wonderful ideas – but you are not holding *now* as a beautiful place to be. It is what you want ahead. You can't go ahead unless you have got *now*. Now is the foundation. Now is not a wishful thing. It is a solid *"I am who I am. I am essence and I am choosing to work with my truth."* The *Spirit*, of course, is truth. It is a feel. It is not a thought, it is a feel.

You know when you are out of comfort with self. You know when you are in comfort with self. Those are your foundations, and it is from here you go, *"My next step is here."* And your next step goes there, and you travel it with care, with great love.

Sharmini: Yes, it happened. I thought I had taken a few steps forward and then I had to come back.

Denny: That's it! I don't think you came back, but I think ego wants you to believe you did. Because you don't do one learning, sweetheart. There are seven levels of it, and I am at the age now where I have given up the thought of ever getting any of them finished. I am working my way through them and might get one or two of the learnings done because they come from other lives as well. But the ones that come at this time – I should be back to do a whole lot of the same work and try and improve on it, which is probably why I am hanging on to dear life!

It is Love and that is the greatest thing I have learned!

There is nothing wrong anywhere. You are in a learning, so you cannot condemn it, which is what you are taught to do. You cannot look at somebody else and go, *"I can't do that but they can and that is not fair."* If you were meant to be them, you would have been, and you would have had all their learnings on top of that.

But actually, you can't be anybody else, so what is the point of trying to compare? You are the perfect specimen. You are what your *Spirit* asked, and you are not honouring it enough. You do have a very difficult time at the moment with Mum and that is time consuming, energy consuming, and every kind of consuming that it can be.

Sharmini: Yes, I have to help her because she looked after me. I have tried to do all the *Marma* points for her and sometimes it works, sometimes it doesn't. I think her mind is in a different place.

Denny: No, she is not where we are. She is at that stage where they oscillate between beta and alpha states of mind. Half the time they are not consciously with you where you want them to be. They are not paying attention, and if they want to fly off, they will. And that is one of the hardest things you have to deal with. If they are in beta, there could be a storm. If they are in alpha, they slow down and perhaps drift. I often wonder if one should work some of the *Marma* points when they are asleep.

What is it that I am picking up on your right shoulder all the time? There is a shortage of colour looking at your aura and it is almost like you are leaking there. Bear with me. It is unusual and has to do with language, or in your case, lack of language. How well were you listened to as a child?

Sharmini: Not at all, because I loved to play by myself. I used to read, and I love reading books, so people always used to say,

"Oh, let her do her thing!" Whenever I said a thing, people never took me seriously. I always had an invisible soul or friend. When I was small, I used to talk to it and my mom would always say, "What the hell are you doing or talking to?" Even now I feel sometimes that I am not being listened to, either with my husband, or even my children, my youngest one. I also tend to do the same thing, and sometimes I also don't listen to people. Now I am making a conscious effort to listen to what you are saying.

Denny: Do you think your thought process was ahead of what was being spoken to you about as a youngster? Could you see beyond what they were saying half the time and chose not to answer because it wouldn't have been understood by a youngster?

Sharmini: Yes, I think so. Yes, I have lost a lot of those gifts.

Denny: No, you haven't! You just put them to rest.

Sharmini: True! I shouldn't say lost. It has just as gone to sleep.

Denny: Yes, but they can wake up now because they can be used the right way. They went to sleep because you weren't strong enough to handle them. You were ahead of what the grown-ups were saying to you and therefore you weren't paying all that much attention. You were there way before they were and when they were starting to talk to you to pass on information, you already knew it, but you couldn't say, *"Well, I know that."*

Sharmini: I know. Sometimes I say, *"Oh my God, has this really just happened? And why didn't I do something about it?"*

Denny: But do you listen to it?

Sharmini: No. I am thinking to listen if it comes to me again.

Denny: Accept that that part of you has a voice all the time. That is your *Spirit* voice, your truth voice from your essence. It is the part of you that is years and years old, and it is trying to understand that there is an essence within each of us.

I try to teach you and all my students how to hear and live on an everyday basis with the inner voice. For example, I don't even eat food without asking my inner voice whether that is acceptable and if my body says no, it doesn't matter how much my head wants it, I won't have it because I am out of my truth. It is that kind of voice, that kind of knowledge, that kind of living, where Love comes in because there is no room for judgement. There is no room for anything else.

The amount of inner work I had to do for me to be able to be of value to others… It never crosses one's mind that you could be doing this for somebody else. You suddenly discover that you are quite useful. You have done a lot of work and you are still there, and it actually helps people. I have been working with people for over forty years now and it is remarkable how I have grown with all of my students and the kinds of people that come to my door now. Well, they don't really come to my door anymore, they come on Zoom or FaceTime.

Sharmini: I would like to work on being more loving to my family and to myself.

Denny: You need to be speaking truth and you need to be you. Just be in your truth and be very loving and gentle with the things you are going through with your mother, because it is so exhausting and ego is dealing with it. Your essence knows, but you are not thanking your being. You need to say. "Thank you for this, thank you for that."

Of course, now and then ego needs to let off steam.

Sometimes I used to drive the car and open the window and yell down the motorway – top of my voice – getting rid of everything. You need to be able to let off steam. Your body – that is doing it all. Your mind – that is listening to your mother. The part that feeds, that washes, that does everything, that beautiful part of your essence needs time out for the ego to recover. It doesn't need any, *"I shouldn't be doing that!"* because those words are banned!

More important is to think, *"Am I being fair to me? How much love have I given me?"* Because if you can't give yourself love and understand that love, then you can't really give it to others. You will only be able to go as far as you can go with your love.

Another example I'd like to share with you:

Imagine me getting very rude with a car driver because of a bit of dangerous driving and I call out, "You bloody so-and-so!" and then instantly I close my mouth and go, "I am so terribly sorry! I don't mean any of that at all," and pull it all back. But it was so instinctive because it was dangerous. Did I come out comforting? Did I come out nicely? No I came out absolutely ego and it was like, *"Oh well, you know, I didn't win on that one but well done, Denny, you saw it."* I will say to myself, *"Well done, I am so sorry I did that but well done for seeing it."* That is a big step forward.

I can see far more colour around you coming up now. Listening to my crowd, my guides, it is as if we have given you permission to do far more than you are doing at the moment to look after you and the world as a whole, but mostly to look after you. Would you agree?

Sharmini: Yes, because looking after me automatically means the world, the surroundings get looked after, too.

Denny: Yes! Whatever we send out comes back. It is a reflection. You have it! It is coming! Honour it, and well done with your mother, you need a medal.

Sharmini: Thank you!

$$\infty$$

Sharmini reflected on her session with Denny in January 2022

- Denny has opened me up to loving myself first.
- To look past all judgements and honour myself and my *Spirit* more.
- I have learned to love myself and others with all their flaws.
- To not be in judgement of myself and others.
- To acknowledge ego and sit with it so that it does not overtake my life.
- Everyone has their journey, and it is important to work on my own journey.
- Developing my connection with my *Spirit* and opening up my intuition.

- It is by doing this we will be in tune with our *Spirit*.
- A journey of a lifetime, which I have started.
- "The Ancient Secrets Community" has been a wonderful platform to connect with the spiritual self.
- With connection with like-minded people, and through *Seva* I have opened up myself more.

"I am who I am. I am essence and I am choosing to work with my truth."

"Everything that makes you who you are is made from Love."

Session #5: Annabelle
(Follow-Up)

You Are the Project & You Are Everything.

Gill: A few weeks after Annabelle's first session, she met with Denny again. Annabelle felt happier with herself and more content. She noticed she was being more appreciative and grateful for what she had.

Denny: You feel as light as a feather today. It shows you how much of other people's stuff you were carrying, which wasn't helping you one little bit.

Most of what I say is channeled, and my guides are still chasing you, which is why they are asking the question, "What can you tell us about you that is different?" Because you see, you are the project. You are everything. You are what matters and, by seeing this, it creates a difference in you as the project. You suddenly realise that you are not a bit of flotsam floating around because you didn't know what else to do. You are actually vitally important in this world!

It is taking you a long time to suddenly realise that *you are the project*. You have come back by *Spirit*, whether you want to or not, in a very interesting period of history where we are all at sixes and sevens, energetically. The planet is moving so fast. We are having to adjust, and an awful lot of us can't. It is too fast; it is too quick.

Spirit is saying, *"You have got to stop where you are, how you are, and start paying attention to how you are living and your reason for being. We haven't chosen to be alive in this time by accident."* You are coming in at the last number of years of the exchange – the great big exchange – doing training, and more training, and teaching love. So that all of those who will take it on for the next generation, really do understand where they are coming from, and see the importance of who they are, what they are, and why they are. And get the sense of, *"I am love."*

Occasionally I struggle with my body, and I am too busy playing ego games, finding fault, because my body is not working very well. But I am not helping me at all. I am attacking me because I can't do this or that. But nobody says I have to. That is my ego having a wonderful dance. My truth is just love.

When I look around your aura, it is getting a richness to it. But there is still a backward step occasionally, where everything is going brilliantly and then you think, *"I can't possibly. No, I am not good enough."* And this is where you backtrack.

Now, the reason we are together is for me to teach you how not to backtrack and to ask you why you are backtracking. The experiences you have had way back – *you,* sitting here – didn't have any of those experiences. The experiences I had in the orphanage and afterwards, I didn't have now. My *early me* did, and it is her pain, her traumas that I carry.

Once we understand that these beautiful earlier versions of us have done all the work to make us what we are today, we start to understand how incredibly, wonderfully lucky we are. If they have survived it, they have done it all. And they are still doing all they can to get closer to the *Spirit* that we really are. They are not hearing enough from you, talking to them as their future, saying things like, *"I am so proud of you."*

Going back to your six-year-old again. Have you sensed her at all?

Annabelle: No, I have a hard time with stuff like that. I think I had a more traumatic thing that happened in fifth grade. I know what you explained about her was that she wasn't being *yelled* at, but she was *feeling* that person. I have that energy in me so much.

I had to learn that when people do that, it is not me. When I am in a class or are at work, managers are saying, "People *have* to do this. They *can't* do that." And I am thinking to myself, *"But I don't want to do what they are saying."* That is one issue that I guess is hard for me to grasp. I guess it is that six-year-old.

Denny: It is the start of a pattern, which you still come up with every now and then. We need to lovingly expose that six-year-old, but very lovingly say, *"You did absolutely the best you could do at that stage to stay safe."*

Look how brilliant you are! That six-year-old is one of the biggest reasons you are what you are today. She couldn't turn around and run. She couldn't have done anything, and she didn't because she didn't know what was going on. She had no redress because she was a child, and she goes on facing that. How many times has she heard her future go, *"My goodness, I am so proud of you!"*

For example:

I created safe inner places for my inner children, particularly from the orphanage days. In my mind we built a lovely outdoor home for all the different ages – when I was in a cot, pram, and crawling and walking, right up to and when I left the orphanage and beyond.

But as I collected my inner children over the years, I found them and managed to teach them what they needed to hear. I did some big learnings in those days where it wasn't what *I* wanted to do for them, but rather what *they* wanted me to do for them.

I think there was a very arrogant part of me back then (30 or maybe 40 years ago). I was giving to my inner child what I thought she needed, which actually made her run away and keep running.

Then I stopped when I had the realisation of what all these youngsters had gone through on my behalf, especially in the orphanage. I eventually realised that this child was the magical me that had gone through so much on my account for me. It was love she needed, and nothing else. The learning of love and belonging, so I gave her so much love.

This was my biggest eye opener in understanding how important it was to feel what *she* wanted, not what *I* thought. Then she just slipped on the floor and fell asleep from exhaustion. She had done so much running from me up to that point.

As I connected to my inner children, I created a special place in my mind, and I collected them bit by bit. There were lovely ancient oak trees and a stream for them to play together. When I checked in with them, they would cry out to me or rush out to me for love, even wrapping themselves around my legs. I have been doing this for years.

They are so happy because they are children again with none of the pain or agony they went through. I was able to hand that back to Mother Earth with great love to recycle. But my inner children have my love and thanks. Without that kind of knowledge and learning, I would never have the gifts I have today.

I have always been psychic, but because I come from a place of love, my ego is out of the way and I can see the whole of you. It is the sheer love of blending with you. In that partnership, we are one, and we have come from the same place – *Spirit*.

We are all Spirit down here, living our story, which will have a definite effect on each and every one of us. My story will have a huge impact on you. Your story will have a huge impact on me. We are never doing it just for ourselves. When we are doing it for us, we are automatically doing it for everyone.

If we think we are trying to do it for others, and we are not in the equation, we are going to fail. Because if we should understand love, and the joy of love, it is not the joy, it is not the parental love, or the child-to-parents love. It is none of those *labeled* love. It is purely love.

Everything that makes you who you are is made from Love.

Because the ego loves to label, and the body is eager, it feels all the pain. It gets hurt really badly. It blames itself so often: *"I have got to be the faulty one. I am not good enough. But if somebody needs my help, yes, I'll go and help him."*

Is it helping you? You haven't had time to notice. You haven't gone looking. Why not? Because you are the project and your *Spirit* set you a whole list of tasks of emotional learning. Have you succeeded in overcoming any of them? Or are you too busy making everybody else better at your expense?

These are the bits I am looking for in you. Are you aware that you matter as desperately equally as anybody else?

The only thing any of us is trying to do when we are back here is remember we are love. And we have every problem, scenario, situation, pain, trauma – you name it – come into our lives that makes it harder and harder to remember that we are simply love. We start to label ourselves, *'not good enough.'*

I had quite a phone conversation with my son last week. He was having a tough time at his job. He kept saying, "I can't do it!" He is a director in a firm, trying to train everybody around him, which he is normally really good at.

He kept on saying, "I can't do it. I can't do it." I could hear the disbanded voice, and I said, "Your language is all wrong.'

His reply was, "But it's absolute truth, Mum."

I said, "Okay, there is your essence listening to what you are saying. You are saying, *'I can't do it.'* So that is the message you are sending out. If you change that sentence and add one three-letter word, it changes the whole format. The word is *yet.* Y-e-t. 'I can't do it, *yet.*'"

One word. He transformed his entire attitude towards the problem. This week, he is dancing. He keeps sending messages saying 'It works! That works! I had a really good meeting. So pleased about that! I am beginning to understand.' Totally different. All it took was to add a little word: yet."

This is so much of what some of your inner children need to hear because they feel they have missed the boat. They haven't. They haven't been loved enough by you. They are not hearing how proud of them you are, and you really do understand that you are where you are today because of them.

Annabelle: I like that story because I am having problems, or I have failed...

Denny: Not failure. You are learning.

Annabelle: Yes, I am learning to do it, but it is difficult.

Denny: You, aged four, you are deeply, deeply upset about something. You are looking outwards at either a relative or teacher, and in that fraction of a moment, all your trust in grown-ups goes out the window. Now, either you have witnessed something earlier, which makes what is being said a lie, or nobody wants to hear your truth, which is distressing for you for not being heard or believed. Knowing that, you will lie because you'll be too frightened to say the truth because you are surrounded by grown-ups. There is a horrendous fear inside you. It is something to do with being left. You are behaving like an adopted child, yet I didn't see you as being adopted.

Annabelle: Funny you say that. I honestly don't know the age, but maybe it was four. I don't remember. I have to ask my mom.

My sister, for some reason, got tired of me. She is four years older than I am. She told me I was adopted, and I said, "I'm not!" She was pointing out everything that was different between us. She is short, I am tall. Her hair is straight, mine is curly. Her eyes are green, mine are brown turning green. I went crying to my mum, "Maya says I am adopted. Is that true?"

She started laughing. "No, no, it is not true." She said, "Maya, why would you tell your sister that she was adopted?"

For some reason they didn't have pictures of me when I was a baby in the house, so we had to take a trip all the way out to our grandparents' house, which was a big deal. My dad's father was a photographer and he had lots of pictures from when I was born. We laugh at that now, but she could be so cruel.

Denny: You don't have a persona. You know what I mean by persona? It's when someone has a mask. You don't have a mask.

You don't have a persona. You present yourself. *"This is me and I am okay with me, and that is all it matters."*

Try following your *Spirit* and not your ego. Ego is your body. Your ego is your lowest form of intelligence. It is doing its best. It is not working against you, but all your experiences are at the ages when you needed them.

Annabelle: I know when you say the word 'ego,' and I know they talked about that on the "100-Days Ancient Secrets" course, when we were tasked to clean the toilets. But I always say, "I don't know what my ego is. I am trying to figure out what my ego is because it doesn't bother me cleaning the toilets." When they say, "You need to let down your ego," I think, *"Hmm... I don't know what my ego is."*

Denny: You can tell the difference between your beloved ego and your truth, which is *Spirit*. Ego always gives you a reason.

Annabelle: Gives you a reason?

Denny: Yes. The *why* to a situation or an answer. Let's say you ask, *"Do I want to go out for tea and cake today?"* Well, that for me, is a safe thing I can say, because you can't move anywhere still in this country due to lockdown. I am on a detox – only moong bean soup – and it is me versus breaking my pledge to getting something to eat 'illegally' when I am not supposed to do that for thirty days. The ego part of me is saying *"Just once, nobody is really going to see."* That is not your truth. Your ego says it doesn't really matter.

Annabelle: Do I have an ego? I am not sure, but everyone talks about their ego. I don't think I have one.

Denny: You have one. We all have an ego because we are in an ego body.

Annabelle: So how do I find that ego to let go?

Denny: You can hear it. You have very little ego *in* you, but understand every one of us is born into an ego body. From an early age we are taught by our parents or our teachers – "You *should*. You *ought*. You *could*." All these wonderful words that I ban all my students from using.

Your truth says a very definite, *"No."* But ego says, *"I need to know why. What am I doing wrong? What am I saying that's wrong?"*

Spirit doesn't have right and wrong. *Spirit* just has the word 'learning' for everything. We are good at the blame game or judgement. This is ego. *Spirit* doesn't know what that means.

For example: Perhaps there is a dress you would like to buy. *Spirit* is hearing you say something like, *"I won't get that dress because I am not going to be able to afford it. My truth is no."*

But ego is going, *"Oh, come on, really, you can."* That little voice is quite the opposite of what you just said. Once you recognise this, you can say, *"I no longer obey you, Ego. I obey my truth which is Spirit. If my Spirit is playing with an emotion, then it is not my Spirit. It is ego. Spirit will not tell you why not to do something."*

Annabelle: I want to help children with disabilities. There are many people that perceive disabled children in a way that is wrong and unfair.

Denny: Take out the word 'wrong.' That is an ego response. Take out the blame game. It is a learning. Instead respond, "*If I appear to be having people sabotaging what I am trying to do, I need to look at me, because I must be doing something that is causing them to have that response.*"

What I am picking up is that you have brilliant intentions. I don't see a gentleness in your approach. You are attacking. "*It is wrong. It is not fair.*"

Now, number one, every single one of us is a *Spirit* down here, on a journey of learning in an ego body with an ego brain.

We very often can get angry and upset and forget that every single one of us is on a journey. You are saying it is not fair about these children. Their *Spirits* know damn well what they are experiencing. Your job quite brilliantly is to smooth things out so things become easier for all. If we meet an opposition that is mucking things up, we need to stop and say, "*I am not here to persuade them because they are on their own journey and Spirit knows what is going on. I am here to show them my truth and my gifts, in the hopes that they will hook on.*"

It is knowing you are doing it for the right reasons through *Spirit* and you are only interested in the outcome being successful, even if that means you have to end up in the picture.

Let's see what ways you have to move forward to get the right people with you. I am getting loud and clear that you need to soften. You are being demanding in what you want and what you don't want. You are expecting them all to fall into line with you, and your *Spirit* is going, "*No.*"

You are doing brilliantly but you are taking into account external things, and you are putting up many brick walls. Too many. "*No, no! Won't, won't!*" which is working *against* you, not *for* you. That is all it is. But it is annoying people because you are not softening the edges and having a real look.

Try looking and listening at what is best overall and where you fit in that overall to make it complete. The other thing my crowd is saying is, *"Learn this, and you could be better."*

If in doubt or thinking, *"Oh I am getting tired of this or that,"* tell your ego to *"Shush!"* You settle down and allow yourself to relax and open up, and ignore the way of your ego.

It is your *Spirit's* way that matters – working with *Spirit*, and being far more gentle with yourself, and far kinder to yourself.

If you find yourself in a fearful place, stop and ask yourself, *"Why am I still walking around carrying those fears? What are they doing to me today? Do I still need them? Actually 99% no I don't. It is habit. I repeat them time and time again, and it's high time that stopped."*

You don't need repeat patterns. You are beyond it. You are a very gifted lady. And yet your ego is getting in the way.

It is knowing you are doing it for the right reason through *Spirit.* And you are only interested in the outcome of your dream being successful, even if that means you have to end up in the picture. We need far softer edges and far more relaxing.

I am getting loud and clear that you need to soften. You are being demanding in what you want and what you don't want, and you are expecting them all to fall into line with you.

Exercise: Listen to Your Truth

- Take no action and speak no words that do not respect you.
- Feel the truth.
- Advice, ideas – let them float around.
- If something doesn't feel right, don't do it.

- Wait till you find out what is making you feel uncomfortable, and until you feel the uncomfortable becoming comfortable, don't do it.
- Because your truth has said no, your truth will make you uncomfortable.
- If you get that feeling, don't do anything without absolute instinctual knowing.

You are being asked to soften on you. You are being asked to pay attention and be respectful to you. How easy it is. Remember how important the word *yet* is and remember to love.

"I am Love.
I might have bruises
I might have wounds
But I am still Love."

"It is meeting Love and Love has no negative emotion. It has empathy, compassion, joy, and Love."

Session # 6: Jayna

Healing the Past, Facing Fear, Removing Shame and Blame Because You are Perfect

Gill: Jayna navigated her way through a turbulent household when she was young.

The household was full of anger and sometimes abuse. This had an impact on Jayna. These early experiences were the basis for a series of traumatic experiences and events Jayna suffered into her teens and twenties. Many years later she met with Denny.

Denny: I love your colour in your auric view. One or two insecure patches, but the overall colour is lovely, and it is deep, and it is truth. I love that.

I am being shown problems that had quite a strong effect on you which seems to have you aged about twenty-two. Something that is still affecting you today or the injury from it, the emotional wounding from it. You have never really managed to trust yourself enough to move it on, but you've built very good defenses which were once upon a time very useful. But they are now in the way of your growth and you moving forward. It is your trust.

Let me continue scanning. I am just having a look. What I am looking for are the injuries that are still bothering the energy structure today. I am being shown you as a child with nothing but eyes, huge eyes looking out at the world. Your whole littleness – you are tiny – and you are just made up of eyes questioning the world. There is also a watchfulness already in this youngster. She is watching. She is not secure, and she doesn't know why she is insecure, but she knows she is not safe.

That has a very pronounced effect on our 22-year-old. It is like an accumulation of all those years of survival. Your ability to cover it up, your ability to pretend that everything is okay, has turned it all inwards. Bless you.

You have carried the can so much yourself. You haven't shared it, you haven't shown what the little girl had to put up with, and I have been shown how little she is. She is tiny. It's just dark eyes, huge eyes looking out at the world as if the world is lying to her. Does that make sense?

Jayna: Oh, complete sense.

Denny: Yes, that is one of the biggest learnings that you are going through. This has coloured your life, all the way through all relationships, and the relationship with you, which is the one that got in the way. It is a very large part of that relationship with you that has gone missing, and I think we need to find her. I think we need to find her and hand her back to you.

Jayna: That sounds so delightful.

Denny: I don't think you yet realise that *you are the project*. That your *Spirit* chose to send you back in this form, as female, exactly where you are, born at this time, to these parents who were part of your choice of the learnings which your beloved *Spirit* did. But I think one of the first things we forget is that we are the project. We are *Spirit* on a human journey, confined in a body. It is the only time that *Spirit* is confined in something, and it is confined in our body.

Our body is the lowest electromagnetic energy that we are and carries all our emotions: physical, mental, emotional, etc. And what has been going on with you, darling, as the experiences have been coming in, is you haven't had anybody to turn to, to say, "What is going on? Can you explain?"

And this little one has survived. She has shown incredible strength to survive, but at a price, and her *Spirit* says she can do it. She will get there. Let's get this little one alright.

She is alright to about the age of two. This sweet child was expected to understand. She didn't get the love that she so desperately needed to say, "You are alright." It seems like you came back with a huge load of responsibilities from previous lives. Looking at what is stopping you from loving you, what is there about you that you don't love?

Jayna: Well, let me just kind of fill you in on some things. You were spot on. At age of two was when I started to see *Spirits*. I had seen them in the home, and I would say, "Mum, why are these people at our home?" And she would say, "There are no people!"

I didn't know. I didn't trust. I thought they were real, and I became terrified. I didn't know how to handle this, and I spent a lot of nights underneath the covers, because I didn't want to see them. So, I would sleep with the lights on. I was confused and didn't feel understood in my family. I was little and I didn't know. Nobody else saw *Spirits*.

Denny: Yes, we always turn around and say it's our fault, because there isn't anybody there to say, "No. You are okay.

We now need to ask why did *Spirit* want this one to be in this lifetime? Why did *Spirit* want you to experience this? It appears that your mother didn't know what love is. Did your father love you?

Jayna: We had a connection. When I was 18, he gave me one of his art galleries to manage. I was full of ideas, and when I came up with an idea it would be implemented, and it would work. It was a beautiful system, very synchronistic.

Denny: How much of that gift that you were able to put into this gallery do you own as *you*, as a gift from *Spirit*?

Jayna: It is so interesting because I don't...I haven't.... When I look at that, it's like a blank. My indication is that anything that I have needs to be given away.

Denny: Really? Well, we have got to reverse that straightaway! You are the project, darling girl. I, Denny, am my own project and you yours.

Your *Spirit* is miles ahead of you. It has laid the path. It gives you free will, which is very kind of it, except I am very good at sailing down the wrong paths in my journey and slowly learning, but it comes eventually.

Number one, the very first thing we take on board, is that the only one, as far as your *Spirit* is concerned, is *you*. You are representing this very beautiful *Spirit*, but you are trapped in this human body, run by an ego that tries very hard to do its best for you, but only will put right what it sees wrong at that age. I keep on being shown this little, tiny girl with these huge eyes. *Spirit* is already there going, Here is the first part of the learning. The little one is full of ego. "It is my fault." Nobody is saying, "It's okay."

Everything has to be fine, or you are lost. When we can't feel our beloved *Spirit* we give our power to ego. We think whatever ego says is right, and we struggle on and on. But unfortunately, whatever the cure was that *Spirit* thought of to make us okay at that time, sticks with you at that age.

Now, I was sent straight to your 22-year-old, and today you are still carrying it. She is still stuck. With this 22-year-old, there is disbelief that she is worthy of love, that she is perfect. The love we are talking about has no ego. It isn't love of ego. It is not love of somebody else – *my parents, my lover, my husband, my girlfriend* – it is none of those.

It is that sense of love of *I am the project, I am it all.* I have been sent back with every gift I need to complete this journey I have been asked to do. I will meet pain, I will meet suffering, I will meet joy and love, though I sometimes forget those quicker than I remember the pain. And our beloved ego does all it can to stop us getting hurt so it closes the door. We'd like to open the door and go, "Hang on. Hold on a moment! I am running my life through *Spirit*, not through ego. I need to meet my *Spirit* and know the difference between the two."

I also call Spirit truth, but that means I love all that I am. I love every single thing about me because it is all part of making me who and where I am today. So much of my learning I haven't done as the woman today, but rather of all my yesterdays. I carry them in me.

When I tried to bring out those from the orphanage times, I got this great big insight that I was responsible for rescuing my yesterday children and making them feel loved and belong. They were me and they'd gone through such hell for me on Spirit's learning.

Again, I can see your 22-year-old who has witnessed something, or something has happened to the 22-year-old which has really coloured a part of ego which is going, *"No, never again!"*

But the never again has gotten in the way, because the 'never again' came from ego, who couldn't cope. And why should it, because it is not *Spirit*, it is the ego.

Spirit can cope, but we need to find a route back to realising you are *you*, the right model. You are absolutely what *Spirit* intended you to be. If you were meant to be anything else, you would have been. You are not. You are a perfect, perfect specimen and you are all of it within you, but you look out too much, darling girl. You are far too busy looking out asking, *"Am I acceptable? Is this okay?"* Instead of *"Are they acceptable to me? What are they doing for me?"*

Tell yourself:

- I am the project.
- I am not here to show them how good I am.
- I am here to show me that I am one of them.
- I am part of the whole and I am a vital part.

There is a wonderful gap in your energy field. It's where I am looking. I wonder, *"How much does she love herself?"* And the answer is, *"There is a little gap. She doesn't really understand what it is my guides are saying."*

Come back to our 22-year-old, she is important. Are you able to share? You don't have to.

Jayna: Yes, I think I need to. I just, I need to let you know, there is a lot of shame. Even though I know that there is a Divine Order.

Denny: You weren't born with shame. No, you were taught it. It is not yours to have in any case. Why are we carrying shame?

> **Gill:** Jayna vulnerably shared with Denny about a series of traumatising events in her youth that gave her guilt and shame. There were several more life-changing experiences in her early twenties that were also traumatising and painful. These experiences led Denny to see Jayna's 22 year old. These unusual circumstances created a strong imprint on her which Jayna rarely spoke about. .

Jayna: …I have so much shame around many of the events of my life.

Denny: Take the word *shame* out, would you? *Spirit* asked you to explore and experience all this. It wasn't by accident; it has been intended. The human part of you and the ego have taken all the judgement that society likes to throw at us. We humans are brilliant – we are taught judgement from birth. We've got to be *better* than or *worse* than or *blame* somebody else instead of taking responsibility. We are also taught guilt, which is a controlling tool. It doesn't matter where you are in the world, guilt is at the top of the list as a form of control. *"You mustn't do that! You shouldn't have done that!"* By the time you get to the age of five you are already riddled with guilt.

I ban the words: *should, shouldn't, ought* – none of my students are allowed to use those words. And I have banned the word *guilt*. Guilt is taught from outside. We never came in with guilt as an emotion. Guilt was taught and we carry it silently, therefore guilt is banned.

Have you ever, ever, heard Spirit talk about guilt? There is only one word that Spirit uses for different learning and that is simply, *learning*. Every experience we go through is simply a learning that we are doing on behalf of the Spirit that we really are.

You have done brilliantly. Your essence had a hard task.

Remove shame, please! You did what *Spirit* asked of you and you made your decisions, I think incredibly bravely. You could have run a mile or buried your head in the sand. You could have done all these negative things and you didn't, you faced it. When somebody learns to face, *Spirit* is watching very closely, because *Spirit* is always with us and when we do a movement like that, *Spirit* knows we have done that jump. But you haven't taken any of that, *"Well done!"* on board. All you do is carry shame. It is not yours to carry.

Exercise: Talk To Your Body

I would love you to incorporate and say to your body:

- My beautiful body, you have done so brilliantly well on our journey so far.
- I can't thank you enough.
- I love you for all you have gone through for me.

Really let your body start to feel *the ages* that went through these experiences. They were so young, and yet they faced those experiences. That shows tremendous strength of will, of love, without you knowing it. All you have done is labelled it as *'shame.'*

You've got to feel that love. You – the *today* woman – didn't have any of those experiences. You – talking with me – didn't have any of those experiences. Your *yesterdays* did. Therefore, you are honouring them. But remember *you* didn't experience it. *They* did. They did it for you. They made the decisions without any support, without any help from anyone.

You went with your truth. You could have been persuaded; you could have buried your head in the sand. You could have followed when someone else said, "Do this or do that." You didn't.

Now look at that wonderful strength in you and own it. Own it!

You are carrying these incredibly brave youngsters that did their best, which was magnificent because they faced. So, we lift a great load of shame out. There is no shame there because that is ego.

Spirit is so proud and so impressed with you. *Spirit* knows what you did, how tough it was. But you, the owner, feel shame because you are living in a world of judgement.

> *We are not here for the world.*
> *We are here for our journey.*

From my own learnings I know that my inner children needed my reassurance that they were loved. They now know that they are loved and the trauma inside them isn't there now. I have had some extraordinary guides that helped me over the years. I always had a collective group. I also had a lot of individuals who suddenly turned up to teach me a particular lesson, at a particular time.

One time there was this really chubby kind of guide, he was like the Michelin Man. He was a real chubby thing, and we sat on a wire. He was just an essence, but often guides put on some form so that you have a vague idea.

Anyway, he was flying me over parts of Earth and pointing out the conflict and horrors, and I arrogantly said, "Isn't it tragic? The hatred and destruction going on down there with everybody killing each other! and giving a wonderful opinion as if I knew it all." The reply came back, "Denny, you are seeing it from your perspective only. Every single person you are seeing there is trying to find their way back to love. Just because you can't see it, it does not mean it is not true."

I have never ever forgotten and when you think of it like that, who are you blaming?

All of those that offended me, or I allowed to offend and harm me, couldn't have done it unless I said, "Yes." I was tiny, however innocent, and my *Spirit* was there every step of the way. It was learning to take responsibility that set up that learning for me.

I was in the picture, as if I was in a video. Then I had to take responsibility for everything that went on. This was my story. It wasn't theirs. They were playing their part that *Spirit* asked them to play. So, there is no blame game. You can't blame anybody. You can't blame yourself because you are in the story. *You are the story,* and you are doing *Spirit's* story to the best of your ability.

I think we give ourselves ten out of ten for turning against ourselves. *"Shame! Horror! I did all these things!"* Completely forgetting that this is ego and human. It has got nothing to do with you.

Jayna: I was looking for love and acceptance and thinking if I could hide those experiences, then I would find love.

Denny: Sweetheart, you can love you the way I am talking, but everything that has happened to you has been with *Spirit's* permission. We take out every emotion except Love. This was chosen. Spirit thinks I can cope. Half of the time I don't feel I can, but I always do because *Spirit* is right beside me. It knows I am doing my best to be just Love, and nothing can attack Love. It is like an electric current.

Exercise: You Go High. They Go Low.

Imagine your essence — your electromagnetic energy — is going to war and war is coming towards you. You are in battle, and they come together, and they crash. It is war.

What does love do? You have an electromagnetic energy coming towards you, something utterly horrible, nasty, not right, coming towards you. You see it. You understand it. You lift up and you go above it, and it goes so fast, and it has got nothing to attack!

So, it stays out over there, and you are completely untouched. You moved, and shifted your electromagnetic field, so that you will not meet up with that. This is a marvellous tool for under-standing that you have your love of you, and only you, and every single part of you is true love.

Then every reflection that you meet, every step that you take, anybody that you meet — they cannot harm you. Because if they come out negative or harmful, *you are not there, you have gone above.* You do not meet. You love them for where they are, but you do not meet up with them again. And anything that would like to come and bang on the door, it can't get in, because it has nothing to fight against.

It is meeting Love and Love has no negative emotion.
It has empathy, compassion, joy, and Love.

If you meet anyone or anything that is jarring, you don't join in because you are out of your truth. And out of truth is ego. Not intentionally, but it's tied up with shame. It's tied up with blame game. It's tied up with *"Oh look at all these things that happened to me!"* No, they didn't. They were laid out for you on your blueprint that you said you were strong enough to have a go at.

No part of you has gone, *"Wow I am brilliant. I am managing. I am growing fantastically through all this. Well done me! Well done to my inner ages – you have been fantastic – and I am fantastic because I am still becoming all that I am. I am beginning to honour and love the Spirit that I really am."* That is love.

There is no blame game. You are learning, and you are learning through love now. All this blame game, what other people think, any of that, you don't need.

You are answerable when you die. When we all go home. It is not a question of what we have managed to achieve on behalf of others or what we have done – that's an ego response. Not interested.

My life, working with people that I love, that is not the issue. When I go home it is, *"Did I manage to learn any of what Spirit sent me back to learn?"* That is all that *Spirit* is going to be interested in. I am not out here to impress the world. But if I impress me, I will impress those around me. Does that make sense?

Jayna: So, how did you make that shift and make peace with all that you suffered as an abused child? I understand the loving of the children at the specific ages, but how did you make that shift? Did it automatically come as you integrated those children into who you are?

Denny: Gradually, gradually, I learned that I had to take responsibility for every experience I ever had, and that was the biggest step. I had to take responsibility for abuse in the orphanage, which was a pretty tough step. But to take that responsibility was the start – and to realise that in every experience the common denominator was me – that started the answer to, *"Why was I there? What was I to learn? Why was I in that situation?"*

And from it came, slowly but surely, a great love of me for what I have managed to survive so far. And a great awareness of the stupidity of blame game – trying to say it is everybody else's fault except mine. I was shown, very lovingly, how utterly stupid that was because there were different players from different scenarios, and I was the common denominator each time. And as that dawned on me so came the lessons:

1. This is my journey.
2. I take responsibility.
3. I love.
4. And I will love this person of me, this part of me that went through this learning for me.

It was the realisation that me, sitting on the sofa here now, did not go through any of those orphanage experiences. I didn't do anything. I didn't stay in this horrendous mental place. I didn't experience any of that. My inner children did. My yesterdays did. And that makes a huge difference, because they all survived. I love them all, but I also love all those that were put in place to play their parts. They are all actors.

Jayna: I didn't realise that was how you made the shift. But I guess if it is divine order, then those children would be put in that place for that experience and could handle it. I have just got chills all over my body.

Denny: Your inner children need loving. They need so much loving from their future, which is you, and they need so much 'Thank-you' and recognition of what they have done for you so far, whatever age. It shows the strength of you and how beautifully strong you are. You have battled through some unbelievable experiences, desperately looking outside for love, validation, and belonging. None of which the child had.

> *I am it all. I only need me. If I fall in love with somebody, I can love them, but I don't need them to make me okay. That is my job. If I love, I will enjoy them. But I am not asking them to be there for me, because nobody can do that for me. Only me.*

It is the gradual understanding of, "I love me. I take no step that doesn't check that it feels okay. There will be a smoothness, a calmness, a gentleness in me, and it will say, "Yes, it's okay, you can do that."

I have been a bit upset over the last two days because I can't walk at the moment. And I am a bit sort of niggly, thinking that it is not fair. It has been trying to raise its head and the typical things that go with pain and disagreement and various things like that, and I had to come each time and say, *"Come on, Denny, you are love. Why are you being so harsh? Your body is doing the best it can!"* because much of the damage to the body comes from my orphanage days which I have carried all my life.

It is the ability to go, *"Okay, it is this beautiful body that is doing it and you can handle it."* And I can. I wouldn't be asked if I couldn't, but I still watch the dear old ego going, *"Oh God, I have put my foot out of bed, and I can't stand up straight today!"*

So, I have to go back and sit on the bed and go, *"I love every single part about me."* And I do.

I think the 'learning to love' stems from, *"I can take responsibility for the child onwards,"* because I chose these experiences and I am, in every case, the common denominator.

The story and the lesson were for me, but I no longer have to do that. That no longer applies today because *I am love.* Can any of those ego thoughts get through? No! I am joy. I am happiness. I am fun. I have my off days like anybody else, but I love the people, and when love really is understood by you, the reflection around you is the same. They are just reflecting you back to you.

Jayna: I love that, because I had that experience yesterday, which was so beautiful. I did give credit to *Spirit.* I didn't take the credit. Now, I will take the credit.

So, Denny, let me make sure that I understand you correctly, because what you have said to me has been so spot on that I want to make sure that I am hearing you right, and hearing you the way that *Spirit* wants me to hear it.

What I am understanding is that with my lack of self-love right now, the foundational pivot point existed at age two, when I made choices and decisions because of being naïve, because I was just a child. From those decisions I made other decisions later on. But as I go back, I am able to heal that child at age two, and at twenty-two, and so on.

Denny: Take away the 'I heal.' You go back and find out what *they* need. Remember, it is what they need from us.

Jayna: It is interesting because my first thought of that two-year-old child is, *"I need to be alone, because alone is safety. And whenever I am in a group, I am unsafe, because I don't know what's going to come at me."*

Denny: Yes. Now, if you start off with her, you are always by her, not interfering with her, just in her presence. You are doing whatever you are doing, but she is there. She can connect with you, or not, but she knows you are there. And she knows you love her. And she knows you make no demands. She can trust your normal behaviour. You don't change. She will gradually turn towards you for safety. Then you will start to find out how best you can love, and she can feel it. And then love just pours in. It is just beautiful.

Jayna: I am going to ask some questions that may not even matter, but it is regarding the mechanics of this. Do I sit down for half an hour a day, or an hour a day, and work with the child, my child?

Denny: No, I just let it occur. When it suddenly occurs, I make no demands because it is the child's timetable, not mine. I can be sitting minding my own business and suddenly a thought will come in and I will stop everything, and go in on that, and allow the child to talk or whatever's going on. Then it has come and gone.

It works beautifully because there is no timetable, nothing organized. It is done through sheer love and when she is ready, when you are ready, it can occur from anywhere. There is suddenly a space were *Spirit* goes and we can use that. We don't put timetables to anything, except love.

Jayna: Such as, put the intention of love, and the intention of openness and acceptance towards that time?

Denny: Yes, and if any age comes in, you start off with, *"I love you. Welcome!"* And then you allow it to flow. Take away your rigidity, take away shame. Shame is absolutely forbidden! It is banned. You have got most of it out. There is a bit around, but it is not yours. So, you are hanging on to something you have no right to hang on to.

∞

Exercise: Sieving Your Body

This is a good exercise for helping you shift perceptions and feelings of the body.

- Imagine a sieve, like a garden sieve that is above your head.
- It is about two feet above the head, two feet out from the body and it has got fairly large holes.
- You bring it down. Right down your body, through your body, right down and take it down to the Earth and you ask the earth to recycle it because it is recyclable.
- You get another sieve, and it has got smaller holes.

- This time you are collecting the gunge that is not yours, coming down on that sieve and you are clearing your entire aura field.
- Then get down, hand it over to earth, thank her and ask her to recycle it.
- The third sieve has tiny holes, and it is the dust, and you are just collecting.
- At the end of it, you are left with you.

There are some times when you might want to do sieving:

1. If you have been shopping in a big store, you will have walked into very many energies which have rubbed off on you, and you come back home feeling heavy because two-thirds of the energies are not yours.
2. If you just walked past an energy where somebody has got a downer. Their energy might have been snapped by yours or caught on yours, and some may even try to unconsciously pinch some of your energies.
3. Of course, if you are uncomfortable with you, sieve.

Jayna: Okay. It's a very good trigger point: *"If I am uncomfortable with myself, sieve."*

Denny: Yes, because nine times out of ten, it is *not* you. But if it stays uncomfortable, it means you are about to take an action that is not truth.

If you are left feeling uncomfortable, it means whatever you were about to do, or an action you were thinking of taking, is a no, no, because Spirit is saying, *"No."* We only know the truth when it feels, *"Yes!"* It feels good.

Jayna: Yes, that feels very good. Thank you!

Denny: You are wonderful. I want you to realise how wonderful you are. I love you.

Jayna: I love you. I am so grateful for your story and your sharing!

Denny: You are a wonderful lady. Go forward. Ban shame!

"It is truth, sweetheart, and truth is Love. Truth is Spirit. Truth is essence. Truth is Love!"

Session #7: Marcus

Always Be in Your Truth & Honour
Your Learning Journey

Denny: So, if I was able to say to you, "Hello, darling man, what subject interests you today?" Would that give you the space and time to feel what does or doesn't?

Marcus: I am in this loving presence, and I am grateful for who I am, and that is what is required in this moment. So that is a beautiful place to be.

Denny: That is a magnificent place to be. *Never compare yourself with others, nobody can, because we are all unique and different characters.*

I was talking to somebody the other day and during a session they were talking about a lack of peace, love, and respect for themselves because they had so many comparisons going on with others, and in their own mind they felt they fell short.

"If you were meant to be any of them," I said, "you would have been them, but you are not because you are here and this is you and this is a model your *Spirit* chose in this period of history, and the changes that are going on. You are in the age bracket that is doing something and bringing on the generation of saving the planet – bringing in love and the new understanding, more and more."

It took ages for the penny to drop that this model was the model that *Spirit* had chosen, and she wasn't meant to be somebody else. The understanding gradually came in that we are absolutely perfect now. Warts and all, funny shapes, anything like that, that is not the issue and has got nothing to do with it. It comes down to answering three simple questions:

1. *Who are you?*
2. *What are you?*
3. *Why are you?*

Working with these three questions sets my clients on a totally different path of opening themselves up to themselves and suddenly seeing, within themselves, how beautiful they really are.

Marcus: Something came up for me when you suggested earlier giving some space for me to speak. I have one area in which I don't quite yet know how to get myself through. I am trying and working on it, and I have one area which deals with relationships and sexuality. Could I just share with you the process that I have been on?

I am trying to figure out if this is in my DNA, or is it me? I grew up in a faith in which I was a virgin until I was married, so there were a lot of hormones. There was a lot of guilt, lots of rules, and I don't think I was guided by love. I was guided by the rules, guilt, fear, hormones, all kinds of stuff.

When I got divorced, only a few years later, I thought, "Oh, what am I left with now?" I always thought I would be married forever. I thought it would be a commitment for all of not only life, but all eternity.

Then I started to look at what do I really want, and when I was finally honest with myself and finally got to that point, I realised that there is no right or wrong. Some people for example have open relationships, but that never attracted me. But just having one partner could never fit in my mind. If I had one partner but was attracted to another person with sincere love, I would attach guilt to it and then it would separate me from my partner. So, it not only separates me from my partner but separates me from myself. Then I thought, "Okay, what is it that I want?"

I don't actually know exactly what I want in this area, but I am just playfully going with it. I feel like my natural inclination is in a world in which it is possible to build something together with several partners. We are all building something together. I can't tell if it is my DNA or my soul, or what it is exactly. I have desires of being with multiple partners, but not random partners, and would love to explore it somehow, consciously, beautifully with other beings. I am not seeing myself as the centre of all the activities. I want them to love each other just as much as they love me and be together beautifully. However, I am not sure.

Denny: You are actually talking about how some tribes live today and how our ancestors lived within their communities. Even children were raised and adored by the whole community. That was how life was and you were held by love and truth. And if it was falling apart because the growth had moved beyond that stage with one of them, then they needed to be able to continue to grow with another relationship.

Marcus: Seems like a healthier way to do it.

Denny: And a happier way! But to get back to that is what we are trying to do. We are *Spirit*. We are the healers. We are the stories, and we are there for each other in every phase of life.

When I hear you talking about having relationships that don't last, it's showing you have been learning and growing until you are ready for your next phase in your life. It doesn't matter whether they are male, female or all these other astonishing terms which have gone straight out of my head.

Who you are is your truth, and if you have given yourself the task to be born in this time with the changes that are going on, even with so much fear in the world right now, it is a magnificent time to be alive. As long as we are seeing why we are alive. It is no longer the simple, easy route that it was before, and as you so rightly say, "I don't know what it is that I want."

Long commitment can sometimes hold us back from our growth, and growth is what we are down here for. At the beginning of the relationship, it usually works wonderfully, and possibly for a few years it is absolutely fabulous. Then things can change and the couple is not in harmony. Not working or building together. Instead, there are disagreements, and they are struggling to keep the relationship going.

One of the things that can happen is being out of their truth, because they are worried about what people are going to think of them if they take a certain action. Good old ego at its best.

A client I had recently said that she always feels that she's being looked at and feeling 'less than.' She fears being found out, or others finding something wrong and turning on her. That has gone on all her life. She actually made a statement along the lines of, "It doesn't matter what I am, or where I am, or what I am doing, I guarantee they'll find me and bully me."

I asked her, "How old are you?"

"I am 39," she replied.

"So, you are still at school being bullied?"

"No, no, no!"

"Oh yes, you are still in school being bullied because you are letting it happen," I said. We went through a list, and I said, "So, you are saying that everybody in that school was different to you."

She thought for a little while and answered, "Well, yes, because they all got on with each other, except for me, and they were nasty to me. So, it had to be me. They can't all be wrong, can they, Denny?"

"There is no wrong here," I said. "Why did they think they could make your life a misery? What were you doing?"

"Well, I couldn't say no. I couldn't say no."

After we worked on this and she returned for a second session, I asked, "Are you still not saying no now?"

Her reply was, "I am saying no, and I am loving it! It feels so strong, and I was so terrified of it before. When I stand there and say, 'No!' I see them backing off and treating me like a normal person. It's as if I just learned this word – no. All my fears went out the window and I became somebody that mattered."

> *It is the ego versus our truth. If there is a negative emotion attached to a thought, then that is darling Ego.*

Another example is the famous phrase: "My back hurts, it's done it again."

"Oh, really? It's all your back's fault. Your back asked to be hurt?"

"No, I don't mean it like that."

"Well, you've just said, 'Oh, my back has done it again.' Who is taking care of the back? Who is taking care of the body?"

"Well, I am, I suppose. I didn't know my back was going to go."

"Why didn't you know? It has given you signs before."

"Oh, were there signs?"

And I said, "How else can the body let us know that it is in trouble? It has to communicate to the captain somehow. It's like a telephone system – when we get hurt, it hurts. Can you hear the telephone: Ouch! We hear the telephone call and do nothing; then we get more telephone calls, and we still don't pay attention to the part of the body that is in difficulty, the part that has already been talking to us, and we still are not paying attention to the fact that it is a part of us that is in trouble. Just shrugging it off as, 'it will be alright', not understanding the body actually is saying, 'I need help!'"

You are evolving brilliantly. You are going to grow quite phenomenally, and it is quite beautiful to see. You are only just learning to hear you and to hear your beautiful body saying, "I am in difficulty. I need time out." Please, less of the "I can manage." You are brilliant at what you do. You can do it and you will do it.

Where you are now is magnificent and I gather you are taking time out soon. Great! So, the healing can start. Be aware of the importance of you, and what other people see in you. What your own *Spirit* knew you would be doing, which would take over an incredible amount of your life, your journey – which now you have under control – and you are waiting for the peace to come. You know where you are going. You know what you are doing.

Let's go back to the simple basics: the need of love, but it is understanding what your truth is that you are in need of. What is going to feed you? Not others. We don't care what others think about us or what their views are!

I want to hear from you how much your sexuality affects your being-ness in your life right now, and how the outside world is allowing you the freedom to go back to a culture that I was talking about earlier. What is that deep internal love that is not being fed?

Can you feel where I am trying to take you gently and lovingly?

Marcus: Yes, I think so.

Denny: No probing, no digging. It is asking your heart, your whole being, to know what you feel like when you have the right love embracing you. Even if it is for a week, a day, a year. It doesn't matter. Take time out. The moment of love is in its truth.

- *How is love expressed by you?*
- *How do you love to be loved?*
- *What makes you safe in love?*
- *What makes you insecure in love?*

You don't have the freedom in love that you have in the work you do. You have done such a phenomenal jump that half of your being still doesn't understand how good he is yet. You'll get there.

There are some serious questions, sweetheart, but you are not being honest with yourself yet. You have an incredible job to do, but you don't live it to make it okay for others. Your healing, your personality, your character, your love – that is the Marcus that the world answers to. Not the human Marcus. He is trying to find his feet and he is trying to find love. You'll find them all, but they have nothing to do with the Marcus of the world, if that make sense.

If you have six toes instead of five, it is not going to make you any different, except here *(points at her heart)*. He knows he is right, and his heart is going, "Forget what it feels like or looks like to the outside world. I am not here for the outside world. I am here for my *Spirit*'s growth. This is part of my *Spirit*'s growth that is flowing beautifully, and it has given me time now for the next bit of learning. Now I have time to look at my sexuality. I have time to look at my lack of trying to have any relationships with anyone, and yet my whole being is yearning."

It needs loving and your beloved's truth knows it. It is waiting for a button, I think. You are getting closer and closer to pressing this button which goes, "The world doesn't matter. This is where my truth is now, and I must stay in my truth." That is, the level of love we can share with others is the level of love we have for ourselves.

You are between the two at the moment. Can you ask the whole of your being to go back to the moment in your marriage when you knew you maybe hadn't got the right answer?

Marcus: Even before I got married, I did sense that it was temporary. I had sensed that it was a part of my path but that we wouldn't be together for our entire lives. Even before we were married, I had sensed that I would learn important things from it, but that it wasn't going to be a permanent lifetime relationship.

Denny: And you knew that?

Marcus: Yes, I knew it beforehand but didn't want to admit it to myself.

Denny: How long did it take you to be truthful in your answer to you?

Marcus: Two to three years.

Denny: It is an extraordinary feeling when we simply move back into our *Spirit's* truth. We have done the learning. It was a learning path which we chose to go into and in those two and a half years, however long, you would have had tremendous learning. But the biggest of the learning there was that if your truth is saying it is not right, you stop immediately what you are doing, even if it supposedly really hurts people or upsets people. That is not what we are here for and that is not what our intent is.

The only reason they are hurt is because it has hit the nail right on the head and they have said, "Ouch!" But it is our truth to ourselves that causes the ouch, not you, and you are doing them a great service, though at the time they don't feel it.

It's like, as a parent, when the children get fed up with you and they tell you what they think of you, and about thirty years later they say, "You weren't too bad then." They look back and decide that maybe some of the decisions were quite good.

It is truth, sweetheart, and truth is Love. Truth is Spirit. Truth is essence. Truth is Love!

That is freedom, once you are back in your truth.

For you to move forward, sexually and emotionally, it has got to go on truth. How do you feel? What is it you are needing? What are you lacking? What are you yearning for? And know it is the truth and that you will settle for nothing less.

With great love – and I never ever tell anybody what to do or what not to do – but I don't think it would be an idea to hitch up and marry anybody at the moment because we don't quite know where you are, and that is okay.

You will need your space around your whole field. Your freedom. I can see your aura. It is a bit too close. It is too tired and that is okay, we can all understand why. The fact that you are standing is a miracle. However, we need to love and take care of it to hold it and you, so you can finish this incredible creation you started. This creation will go on and on forever, while you get your life balanced, which is as important as the work you are doing.

You are as important as the work you are doing because, without that knowledge, you will never produce that level of work that you are going to be producing and you are vaguely already producing it. That will only come through your love of yourself and a deep understanding of the love that Spirit has already shown you. The greatest gift of all is of course that it knew all along that this job was coming to you and you'd be able to do it, but it shut off a lot. I am delighted your sexuality is coming back because it means you are living, you've got life, you've got space now to feel other fields. It is so important, but it has to feel right, and if there is a single hint of, 'I am not comfortable,' then you stop and wait until you find out which part of you isn't comfortable.

Let me tell you the most extraordinary, ridiculous story but it will actually convey all this. I worked with a lovely guy up in Scotland and he is a creator. He plays with engines and water, and he is a very advanced and extraordinary guy. I have been seeing him on and off as a client for many, many years and I have gone through most of his career with him. I have learned so much about engineering, it is unbelievable, and we were dealing with one of his machines because he exports all around the world.

He got it all set, everything was right, and he checked with his *Spirit* that it was all fine, but it came back, *'No.'* He could not work it out. It didn't matter what he looked at or what he did, he could not find why *Spirit* kept saying, *"No, that is not the answer."* It all worked, and he couldn't understand why he got a no from *Spirit*.

So, I had one of his SOS phone calls and he said, "Denny, I am being creative, but I can't ground it. Can you tell me what is going on?"

"I can't tell you," I said. "You have to go inside yourself. Go into the machine and ask it. It all has the intelligence. It's been put there by man, by thought."

In he went, and he was a really angry, typical inventive kind of being. It took four sessions in the end before he suddenly said in his Scottish accent, "I don't believe it, I just don't believe it!"

"Don't believe what?" I asked.

"It's a flipping screw. It is a tiny little screw in the machine over there that is going to break unless we change it. Otherwise, it is going to wreck the invention."

"Okay," I said, "find a different screw. Do something about it."

And he did. He found it. He put it in. He checked with his *Spirit,* and what was the answer? "Perfect, now get on with it."

His ego was doing everything it could to make him accept that what he is doing was okay, but truth wouldn't let him, and then I wouldn't let him. *Then* he saw the depth of truth. His *Spirit* wasn't going to say, *"There is a screw that is not working."* That was his ego's job. *Spirit* was saying, *"There is something not right."*

"Go and find it" is your ego's job. This is the part that you are evolving at the moment. But so much has gone on in this last year, that emotional parts of you have got left behind.

It's okay, but realise they only got left behind because they are beginning to free you up time to really lovingly look at you and find out what your beloved being needs, feels, is desperate to have. If you work with *Spirit* on it, *Spirit* will bring the players, will bring the needs to us. When we own the truth, when we say, "I am all over the shop facing challenges," give it time, and admit you cannot do it yet.

This is where you are, sweetheart. It is there, but you are not quite ready for it yet. If I ask you a personal question: Are you happy with your sexuality?

Marcus: I feel at peace in most areas of my life right now. I feel happier, more at peace. My short answer is yes, and I am being curious and playful and moving forward with innocence, my own innocence.

Denny: Which is a wonderful tool. It is something not to worry about. It is something to understand, that space is coming in for these thoughts to come back, because they are not new thoughts, they all got pushed away, way back over the last few years. Now life is slowing up enough, or calming enough to make some space for you to come back in. This is you. This is your truth about you. Let your *Spirit* know, "Come on, I am alive and kicking. I have got space. I have this issue now, please help. I can't do it on my own." Well, you can because they are all around.

Marcus: Thank you, Denny. I want to thank you for inviting this space and time to go deep into this love of self and helping me to look at different angles and different ways.

Denny: My honour! As you go away from here, please love yourself in such a way that while we look at all the nightmares we have, all the sorts of things we think that we are going through, all the experiences that our beloved *Spirit* is asking us to study, please remember what we are. And that the ego, the body, the ego thinking, our lowest form, carries all the pain of learning.

Spirit has set it all up. And if *Spirit* put it there, we can handle it.

We are strong enough to find our way through. But we don't push and shove. We somehow try and sit back, even when we have a tough time. It is no different for anybody else having a tough time. It is surviving it, understanding it, and learning through it. And trying to be nice while you are doing it.

When life is tough and I am really uptight about something because I have got pain everywhere, I will say, "Love, love, love, love, love, love, love, love, love!" like that to myself. I say to myself, "Remember what you are," and it swings me back.

Honour this wonderful man, please, and realise that he is healing enough for the Marcus in all of him, and all that makes him is coming back to life.

Alright, darling man, beautiful soul, love you so much!

Marcus: Beautiful. Love you so much. Thank you so much.

"We are going to start to work with Love as the tool, the one and only tool, to bring us to what we are doing down here and why we are down here."

Session #8: Aurora

Self-Respect, Learning, Forgiving Because You Have Got It All in You

Denny: Let's have a look at your energy. Your energy structure gives up the impression of an adopted child. I don't think you are, but I feel it when part of your being shows a separateness between you and the family, as if what you are doing with your life is not understood or accepted properly. Nothing is working with you in their eyes, and they won't listen. How unusual, but it is sad.

No! What I said is incorrect! When I get something and it is not said correctly, I get tapped on the back of the head by my crowd, my *Spirits*, who say I haven't worked with it correctly. When I ask, "Has your family ever really supported you?" I get, *"No,"* and, *"She has always walked alone because there has been nobody there to listen or to understand."* Does this make sense?

Aurora: I understand this completely.

Denny: We need to change that. We need you to turn around, face this and say, *"I am absolutely what I am meant to be. You can be as critical or as serious as you want to be, but that doesn't change who I am. It doesn't change who I am becoming, and it doesn't change the fact that I know I am Spirit having a human experience. I am not a human having a Spiritual experience. I know I am Spirit and I live, to the best of my ability, through truth, through love."*

181

You don't need to live in the ego world of your beloved family. The ego world is made up of our humanness because the body is human. It is the ego body. It is the electromagnetic energy that carries emotions which is the heaviest energy. We are down here to learn how to move beyond the need for emotional pain and the wounds that we get from ego.

Aurora: It has been a ride.

Denny: I would think, it has. But has it made you stronger?

Aurora: Yes.

Denny: It could have made you weaker. It could have made you run away. It hasn't done any of that and one needs to say, *"Thank you,"* when you are ready. Not yet, but one needs to be able to say, *"Thank you,"* to them. *"You have given me the power to turn around and go. It doesn't matter where you are coming from. I honour where you are, and I honour where I am coming from, and that is more important."*

It is the sudden realisation of how much you are being heard outside of your family, how much you are actually being heard. But you won't go very far because you are frightened that you'll be found out if there's anything wrong or faulty or something similar. Things that were thrown at you when you were younger. You are still playing some of those games, so now is the time you are going to have to stop it.

The first thing I see is your parents coming in, walking around you, looking quite agitated with a conversation. You are eight and feeling alone, if that makes sense. This little girl is understanding with a deep awareness, at that age, that she is not heard and so is not mixing. She is trying to find someone to communicate with, but there is nobody that is understanding where she is coming from, at the age of eight. One of the emotions I am looking for, or feeling, is laughter, joy. Where did this child learn that?

Aurora: I didn't.

Denny: No? Why didn't you? What were your parents doing that stopped this child from laughing and loving?

Aurora: I think everything you have said is so exact at this point. I was the first child. I was the one that was treated the most strictly, and I was the one they thought did everything wrong. I was the one that was punished and was the one that was at fault for my parents' fights. I was the reason for my sister's bad behaviour. I was to blame for every dysfunction in the family and, I knew and believed, it was around eight. I knew that I couldn't get love from my parents, so I stopped asking for it. I separated emotionally from them from then on.

Denny: Yes, isolation.

Aurora: You know, if I was going to cry, I locked myself in the bathroom to cry at age eight! I was not going to show them any emotions from me at all.

Denny: The picture they are showing me – my guides are around and connecting to yours – I have been shown your mother was auditory to voice level. She could understand only through voice. Basically, *her* voice, and she would drown out the other voices. She would not listen. Your father was a mixture of visual and auditory. As long as he saw, he was okay. If he couldn't see, he panicked and that is where a lot of his fear came from. Whereas your mother dealt with it with a firm hand and in a derogatory sort of way.

But I am not worried about them. It is what they have done to their daughter and their other child, your sister. What did your inner child do, feeling all this, aged about eight – although I have gone back to age six, because it's taken two years to build to the level of eight – when she gave up?

Aurora: I became really defiant. You know, they said, "Yes." I said, "No." I just wouldn't agree with them on anything. I shut down emotionally. Completely shut down. I would not show them anything. They couldn't give me love and I asked to be adopted.

It was like, "Please put me up for adoption and I can go and live with my uncle." I felt I loved my uncle, and he loved me, so could I go live with him. But I could never run away because I wanted to torture them in a way, as much as they tortured me. With me being there, they were more tortured. I was a source of discord and I liked to see them punished.

Denny: Do you still have that view?

Aurora: My father is deceased. He has been gone twelve years now. My mother is alive, but I didn't talk to my mother for many years. She is 90 now, has Alzheimer's, and I speak to her occasionally. When she loses her memory and can't communicate with me, it relieves me of a need to communicate with her. But when I do talk to her, because of her short-term memory loss, I have been able to tell her all the things she did wrong by me. I am able to take it off me and give it back to her, and within minutes she doesn't recall the conversation, so I have been able to release it.

Denny: Excellent. We are going to stop here. We are going to go into the first lesson that is so important here: *We are going to start to work with love as the tool, the one and only tool, to bring us to what we are doing down here and why we are down here.*

Love becomes a very interesting word. It is not the love of a child, husband, wife, etc. Those are all separate loves. *It is love of self.* We are taught from the moment we can put coherent sentences together, that we are not allowed to love ourselves. *"How selfish can you get? How dare you think of yourself like that! You have to think of others! Don't be so selfish! Don't be so this, don't be so that."*

Let me give you an example:

My mother, who was one of my greatest teachers, said, "What am I supposed to introduce you as, if we meet somebody? What is it that you do?"

I said, "I teach people about love. I teach people what they really are so that they can look after themselves and, through their knowledge and love of themselves, link the world to becoming that level of love."

Straight back before she even had time to think she replied, "Well, how selfish can you get?"

I replied, "It is not that kind of love, Mum. It is not, *'I am love, please world, see me.'* It is, 'I am a mess, I've got warts, and corns and you name it, and I can't walk all over – but I love every part of me that is on this journey on my behalf. And it is *my body* that suffered too much, in my case, and I owe my body the great love for what it has done for me, and what it is doing for me.'

The next day my mother said, "I decided to call you a therapist, is that all right? I just can't work with all the selfish stuff you are talking about, because you always were very selfish."

I said, "That is fascinating. Tell me more."

She cited time after time after time when I wouldn't do something because I knew it wasn't right and I wouldn't go against my truth, which of course was a major sin because it meant I went against what my mother was saying. My stepfather didn't have much to say at all about this, but he was a lovely guy.

It was a realisation that we were all brought up to judge each other, to find fault with each other.

Our peer group – we had to be acceptable. Our parents – we had to be whatever they wanted. How we were behaving had to be acceptable to them, otherwise we were embarrassing them or letting them down. And it was all our fault. As you quite rightly said, "If we didn't do what they wanted us to do, it became all our fault."

When you choose parents like that, it is probably one of the toughest ways you could have chosen to walk. It usually means a very old soul takes this path, as a young soul might never manage it. You become very aware of where you have let yourself down by playing the blame game on you.

Important Reminder

- You have always been perfect.
- You always will be, because *Spirit* chose you to come back down here into a human form to learn what *Spirit* cannot do when it simply is *Spirit*.
- *Spirit* hasn't got a body. It cannot feel emotion.
- *Spirit* just is love. It just is truth.

We live in a body which is made up of ego experiences. It feels the physical, mental, emotional and spiritual. We've forgotten what we said we'd have a go at doing because it has been wiped out of our memories. It is so unkind because, I think in actual fact, if we knew what was going to happen, we wouldn't come back. We would say, *"No, thank you, I'll catch a different bus!"*

Denny: When you were left to your own devices with no assistance, how did you go about it?

Aurora: I became really strong. I have recognised, in the last five years, tremendous amounts of growth. But I recognise that all the things that I got in trouble for as a child are the ultimate things that have given me the strength to live my life successfully and independently and made me able to get through everything.

I have had lots of illnesses. My husband passed away 15 years ago. I married a man who got sick the day we got married and never got well again and died. It is sort of like I keep getting these major challenges. I had a tumour, and other illnesses associated with it. I have had one challenge after the other, and I persevered through the whole thing. I worked my entire life until I retired a few years ago.

Denny: You have grown so strong to survive the illnesses, which means you have a lot you need to be doing. You used the word retire, well, 'bad luck!' (laughs)

Aurora: I retired so I can do what I love. I work more now, with joy and appreciation.

Denny: You have been born at the most critically important time in the world, because planet Earth's vibration has lifted. If you look at our language involving healing, all these words are normal now. But if you go back ten years or more, you didn't use those words. The speed with which these words are now recognised! And the result is that everybody that is living on Earth, that has life – it doesn't matter how tiny or how big – everything that has life is in the new vibration, and all are having real difficulty in maintaining that vibration.

Your *Spirit* has chosen this time for you to be here with all this work going on, with massive change going on, with your illnesses behind you. Your preparations are in place. You are on the path, the right path.

What we are being asked to change in you is your belief that, *"I won't be heard, and they won't believe me,"* which is getting in the way of you being absolutely honest and truthful, and saying, *"This is what I have learnt and know, and I can share it with you."* Then you will be heard.

We are supposed to vaguely know what our journey is about, but we don't. We start to learn by the wounds we get, by the bruising, by the experiences we walk into, and we build the fences to survive. The only trouble with the ego learning at that age is your little eight-year-old has far too much to say in your life today. Still, she needs to be able to hear you say, *"I want you to be out."*

With all my inner children at the orphanage, *Spirit* showed me a lovely magical place that had lots of trees and was a magical sort of child's place. And all my inner children, bit by bit, as I got them out of the orphanage, they began to breathe and live and learn what love was. They discovered what safety was, and remembered what a child was. And then realised how much they had missed.

Originally, when I first used to go back and talk and play with them, they came towards me. They couldn't get enough love, but now they are too busy playing. They are all now children at that age minus the anguish, the pain, the cruelty, because I took all that on board, and I was able to let it go.

After letting it go, what do you have in its place? What are you left with?

Aurora: Love.

Denny: Yes. There isn't a blame game. *We cannot accuse anybody of anything because the common denominator in each experience is us.*

Aurora: I have a question: One of the ways that I chose to stop the hurt was to cut my family out of my life: "I will not let you do this to me again." I haven't talked to my sisters in ten years. I barely talked to my mother, and I do feel much better for it. But then I feel that I get judgement from people around me.

Denny: Every experience you have had, you must be able to face it, understand it, work with it, heal it and learn to forgive. But remember, there is no demand in anything. Love is love. It is the most powerful energy to nourish.

Exercise: She Goes Low. You Go High.

If you look at me and you look at my hands, there is electromagnetic energy.

- Okay, let's say this right hand is you – alive and active – and you are walking along. And the left hand is your mother.

- The left hand is getting ready for a fight, wants to boss, dictate.
- The right hand goes, *"Oh God, it's Mother, what do I do?"*
- You come closer and closer together and you are both on the same vibration. Right?
- So, you meet and the arguments, the fights, the hurt, the pain, the tragedy unfold.

Now try coming from a place of love:

- You are both walking towards each other, and you know exactly what your mother is like.
- You know she is seeing you, and she is waiting to confront you and show you up.
- What you say this time is, *"Yes, that is Mother. I am not prepared to have a fight or anything like that."*
- As you get closer, she could come in and bite.
- Coming from love, you raise your vibration, and get up above her and continue your journey up there in the sunshine.
- Now your vibration has gone up, and hers is on the lower vibration trying to find you to pick a fight.
- There is no need for war.
- We only need to change the energies just for that short time.

So, if you love you the way you should – sorry, I am not allowed to use the words should, ought, or guilt – because guilt is taught from the outside. You are taught that you *should* have done this, you *ought* to be doing that. It is a behaviour that we are forced into obeying by our parents, and we grow up with guilt, and we own the guilt as ours.

No, we weren't born with guilt. We are born with all of those once we came into the body, they were all there sitting idle, waiting for us to grow. But if you look back at your life and see how much you ran, or you still run today, I am being told, it's through guilt, feeling guilty, when it is not your guilt at all. *"I don't want to offend."* Well, who said you were going to?

Your truth might offend, but that was not your intent. So that is their stuff. When you actually see the truth, you see that the only thing we are being asked to aim for – once we are back here on that whole journey before going back home – is to find love at a level where all we can offer is Love. There is nothing soft about us, there is a great toughness, which I like seeing in you, but it's a gentle toughness.

What I am not seeing in you yet is the incredible respect you have for yourself. I am not seeing enough of that. You are not respecting yourself the way you need to. Tell yourself, *"I am it all! I was born with it all! I will die with it all! I am it all the way through my life!"*

You keep forgetting because you are so busy having these experiences that make you feel less. You forget you are whole. You forget you are complete. You forget that you are love because that is where you come from. That is what *Spirit* is, and so they are chasing you, darling girl, because they are saying you have got so much experience behind you already with what you have gone through.

This is your journey, and it can be very, very painful if you don't respect yourself and understand that you are everything your *Spirit* wants you to be. You are doing all the learning your *Spirit* asked you to learn. You struggled, you fought, you are being isolated, and you still carry it. So, friendships – going towards people – is not a natural thing to you, but you are

learning, you are getting better. And you are beginning to realise that you are the one that matters. You don't have to make it
okay for them. You are not there to make it okay for anybody,
except for you.

Let's say you and I are husband and wife, and I love you tremendously, but you actually don't love yourself. You only love
yourself to a certain extent. The rest of you finds faults. You
can only take the level of my love as far as your love for you
will go. If my love tries to go beyond, you say, *"That is not true
because I can't feel it."* And so you attack the one loving you more
than you love yourself, and that is when you start the break-up
of the marriage.

In couples therapy, I found that when you get a hold of the one
that doesn't love themselves and start showing them *where* they
don't love themselves and that they are sending out the message,
"I don't love me, I am hopeless, why should anybody love me?", they get
such a shock when they see it.

Would you be attracted to that kind of energy coming from
a person? No. Well, that is exactly the message you are sending
out from you, that eight-year-old girl who was so damaged and
so hurt, but strong enough to say, *"I'll get back at you!"* And in
her strength, she probably went too far. That is okay because
that is in the learning. It is not wrong or right. It just is and *Spirit*
calls it learning.

The person who is attacking you is you. What gives you the
right to attack you, when what you really are is *Spirit*, who would
never dream of attacking you? Look, *Spirit* loves you. It knows
you are learning. Easy to look back now and say, *"Oh yes, wow!"*
But at eight, she did the best she could for survival and you are
not saying, *"Well done."* You are not saying, *"I am so proud of how
you coped."*

The *me* of today can put things right. Your eight-year-old needs to know how brilliant she was, how much she put up with, and you never said, *"Thank you."* Your eight-year-old needs a medal.

When you feel ready, you need to forgive your parents. It doesn't matter that your father is dead. It is talking to them through meditation, but on your terms, not theirs. It is learning how to talk to them. Not in a dictatorial way, but in a loving, rather beautiful way, using an exercise that I teach a tremendous amount.

Exercise: Parcels

Here's a way you can actually return a lot of the nasty things your parents have left with you.

- Let's say we have two parcels, and two areas, and there is a fence in the middle.
- On one side of the fence are your parents and on the other side of the fence is you.
- You pick up one of the parcels and you look at it and see *Anger* or *Unfair*, or whatever that parcel is made up of. It is something that either your mother or your father gave you by their behaviour towards you.
- You hand it back over the fence and you say, *"Thank you very much for the learning of this. I have learned everything I needed to, and I am now able to hand it back to you because it is your property. Thank you for the loan. Thank you for the learning."*

- They take it back. Sometimes they don't take it back very gently because they can see what they are doing. Others take it back very sweetly and say, *"Yes, we are learning."*
- You give every parcel that is theirs back to them and you get lighter, lighter, and lighter.
- You had been carrying all their baggage and now, suddenly, you are just carrying yours.
- It is now much easier to see what is left of you.

Denny: You are so close to all of this, but you need to be much more gentle, much more loving with yourself. There is a lot there for you to work with, and you will be able to do it! God bless.

"I am it all! I was born with it all!
I will die with it all! I am it all the way
through my life!"

"You are everything you are meant to be. Your Spirit is made up of absolutely everything. Everything that lives, we have a touch of it within ourselves. It isn't just our humanness, it's animals, birds, and plants. We are part of it, and it is part of us."

Session #9: Erica

Love Yourself First Before Loving Others
You are Love!

Denny: What exciting things are we going to discuss today? What are we here for?

Erica: I was just going to go with the flow and see what comes up. I am doing this long dull detox and some emotions have been coming up. Sometimes I feel very lonely, I guess. But I knew that when I listened to you speak, when you spoke about love and how we are loved, that I just wanted to speak with you.

Denny: That is the hardest task from being born: coming into this body, where the essence is now curtailed within the body. If you think that before that, it was free. It could go where it wanted to go, but now it's as though it's curled up within the body. The body is an electromagnetic energy. It can express and experience emotion, which is why *Spirit* uses the body to learn what it feels it needs to learn to progress on behalf of *Spirit*. So, our essence has said, *"Yes, fine."* Of course, our beloved ego, our humanness isn't there. It can't say, *"No,"* or *"Can I do something different?"* which I think is very unfair.

The decision is made, and you are born. You have chosen your parents. You have chosen your gender. *Spirit* has chosen exactly what *Spirit* wants from you, and the kind of the experiences and emotions it would like you to feel, to see if you can move beyond them until the only thing you end up feeling is love.

197

The essence of Love is beautiful beyond words. And when living within Love, there can't be any negative thoughts. It is quite extraordinary.

The first thing you must do is learn to love yourself. Life, of course, introduces lessons that can cause negative thoughts – through parents, school, etc. So, it is undoing those. The most serious one is judgement, because we are so brilliant at judging ourselves against others and finding ourselves not good enough. Or frightened that friends are going to say, "You are not good enough."

But we should ask, *"Why should I be worried about them? They are just another edition of me on their journey. They are doing their learning that Spirit wants them to do, so I don't have to know or understand what it is they are doing. All I have to do is feel my truth. Do I feel this is okay? Am I making a judgement on what somebody else is doing?"*

It is learning that *the feeling* is absolutely everything because you feel this life, the human life, and your *Spirit* can then go on.

Whenever I make mistakes, I always start off with; *"Oh gosh, I have done it again. So sorry, me. But well done, me, for seeing that."* And my body hears it. I am not cross with it. I am not attacking it. I am saying, *"Oh, I have done it again, but this time I have seen it. I am so sorry, me."*

So, we are undoing so much of what we were taught as young ones, and the love that is inside us doesn't really get the chance to show itself in a natural state once we have moved beyond being a baby. Once we are toddlers and beyond, the rules start to come in. You really have to look back at the amount you have to undo, to begin to find that you really are made of love.

So *many* questions: Why are you beating yourself up? Where did you learn to find yourself so faulty? With your love growing for who you are, what are we going to do? Why have you been born at this time – in this history – which is so unbelievably interesting, different, and a huge, massive change? Why are you here? What does your essence want of you?

You are everything you are meant to be. Your *Spirit* is made up of absolutely everything. Everything that lives, we have a touch of it within ourselves. It isn't just our humanness, it's animals, birds, and plants. We are part of it, and it is part of us. We are brought up being told we are separate, but actually we are part of the whole. I live my life as part of the whole to the best of my ability.

When we find a partner and we feel we are doing well together, but then the partner hurts us badly, we can become very, very lost. I believe your beloved *Spirit* is trying to show you that you tried to make it perfectly good, well, and lovely for your partner, but not for you. You fall over backwards to make it right for him, but he takes advantage of that. Why are you doing this?

Erica: In the past, I have done that. I am not with anybody now. I am not sure why I do or did that.

Denny: What was the original thought?

Erica: I am not good enough.

Denny: Yes. Well done. We have to reverse all of that, sweetheart, because if you learn to love all that you are, there is no ego involved. It is not, *"Please see me, I am wonderful, I am marvelous!"* That is coming from our human ego place. It is responsible for keeping you safe. Your ego is doing its best, but because it doesn't change the age of an experience, it becomes a pain in the ass, in polite language. Because if you are doing something at 27, and your behavioural response is that of a five-year-old because something happened to you at five, and your whole body locked itself back as a five-year-old, you are completely lost at 27 years-old.

It is being able to stop in your tracks and say, *"What am I doing? I can't accuse that person of that because using a blame game is me running away from saying, 'I need to look at me in all this. What am I doing? Or what am I not doing?'"*

We usually find when relationships go bang in the night, that somebody has given far more to the other than they should have done and gets almost disrespected for it. They give everything, but it is not really appreciated, and that is because you have given too much. Why are you giving anything other than just you?

Erica: You are so spot on. I guess I was worried I wasn't being loved.

Denny: That means you didn't love *you*. Yet you are absolutely what your *Spirit* wants you to be. You are perfect at birth. You are perfect at death. And you are perfect in the middle.

Spirit is trying to keep you aware that you are loved all the way through, with all the experiences going on trying to disprove, plus, add your teachings – your learnings in school, from home, from parents, from society. What kind of child has emerged? A child feeling, *'I am not good enough,'* forever having to compete.

We haven't got you in the picture – we have got all sorts of emotions – but we haven't got this beautiful lady standing here saying, *"This is me and I am making no apology for it."*

I mean, if I was somebody emotionally important to you today, what would you be saying to me to try to keep me interested in you?

Erica: Oh, to keep you interested in me? Um, I... Oh, to keep you interested in me. Um...Oh...

Denny: You'd be short of words to start with.

Erica: Yes! Short of words. To keep you interested: I am a fashion designer and teach teenage girls about fabrics and sewing, which I have been doing for about ten years. I am the eldest daughter, and I grew up with my mom, a single mother, and we worked as a team together. I have dreams of having a family and having children.

Denny: They are all there. It is a question of whether you are going to bring them in early, or later. It depends very much on whether you can understand that you are it *all*, without apologising. So, when you are meeting people, falling in love with people, or anything like that, you are not asking them to make your life okay.

You would like them to share your life with you. Nobody else is on this planet to give us our life. This is where a lot of relationships fall down. *"I expected him to look after me. I expected him to do this, or her to do that,"* and we are left with them saying, *"Why? Why is another human being sent down to look after you?"*

That is your interpretation gone completely wrong. The only person that can look after you is yourself, and that is your job. And that means you start off by loving everything you are.

We have detrimental emotions like anger, jealousy, hurt, pain, and depression. I can't think of any more, but they are all there and they are all weights of emotions. We can't see the heaviness, although I can see them, but sometimes we feel lighter as we let go of them.

Think of them as energy shifting in different parts of the body – which is why we have body aches and pain as we get older. We are being asked by the *Spirit* to start the programme again of finding love, getting back to what we really are and putting us into situations early on that may be hard to deal with. We can get hurt and bruised and *Spirit* says, *"We want you to move beyond that now."* If you love everything you are and know it is your job to look after you, that nobody else is there to make your life okay, you can share your life and have a wonderful time sharing. And nobody ruins it, except you.

You are going to find people reflecting that back to you, and you will find you are going to have different kinds of boyfriends and different kinds of relationships, where you find that you are not looking at them to make you okay. You are looking to them to have a thoroughly lovely life with walks, outs, dances, films, working together, and whatever you are doing, but loving you for you.

You are not expecting him to make your life okay. You take that responsibility for yourself, and you stay with it and so does he. He takes responsibility for looking after himself.

I see so many breaking marriages which we can sort in time. They are breaking marriages where one of the couple loves the other a lot more than loving themself. It's out of balance. If you love them more than you can love yourself, you then think something is wrong with you.

Do you find faults with them? They are on their learning path. I know it is a very difficult and painful subject, but you can understand it. It is in your whole being – and looking at your auric field, there is sensitivity, and it is getting much stronger, but it is still not owning itself and being its truth. It tries very hard to make a good case for everybody else.

Erica: Yes. I think it might have to do with my dad, who left when I was a teenager. My mom wasn't very well, so I stepped into the role of helping out and supporting financially from a very young age.

Denny: If you go back to your nine-year-old? What went on at nine?

Erica: At nine? We had just moved to Liverpool. I remember at that time having some breathing problems, and the doctors thought I had asthma, but I actually didn't. It had something to do with nuts. My mum and dad were having problems at that time.

Denny: It's somewhere around that time when you stopped believing in you.

Erica: I remember we went on holiday, maybe it was more towards ten, but I might be confusing some ages. I have a memory of being forced to speak with my dad about something. My dad wasn't very close to any of us, and my auntie was forcing me to go and talk to my dad, and I didn't want to. I didn't like being forced. I know that my dad used to show care by buying things for my brothers. He was closer to my brothers and sisters and used to hold the door and greet them.

He wasn't ever like that with me, and I kind of just accepted that my dad was like that, but I always wondered, why? I have spoken to him about it a little bit. There was a particular game he wanted to play, which I didn't like, and on one occasion I basically told him, "No." I told him with a very strong voice. After that he hardly ever spoke to me again. He still remembers it to this day, because I mentioned it to him and said, "I noticed that you didn't really speak to me much after that." He agreed and remembered it too, and just holds a grudge, I guess.

Denny: He holds a grudge because you wanted to do something else.

Erica: I didn't want to play this game... It wasn't nice.

Denny: I totally agree. That is where the grudge comes from.

Erica: Yes.

Denny: He didn't like that. He got beaten by his daughter who made enough noise so he couldn't do it.

Erica: Yes.

Denny: So he becomes what you call a weak man in his eyes because this little, tiny daughter stopped him playing. You know what I mean? But here again, even in that description, as you are talking, *"I'm not good enough"* comes in. I'm seeing your nine-year-old saying, *"I am not good enough."*

Let's look at when you were seven. This is when you really decided you weren't good enough. I think this really started to massively show from the age of 12 onwards and it became a real struggle that didn't get easier.

You gradually learned to bury it. A lot of that is around you today, ready to come up to be sent on its way packing. Because there is a different vibration that is saying, *"You don't need this old stuff, you are not using it."* It is yours, but it is something you haven't played with, used, or needed. Therefore, it can go. Because that piece of energy with that emotion is sitting somewhere in your body – often it is the back – and you suddenly register *that* place has started to hurt. What you then find is that the energy that used to sit there in the body has been cleared out, because you no longer think like that.

"I am whole. I am complete. I am in love with me," would completely take out, *"I am not good enough."*

"I am not good enough," sat in your body for ages, and that energy has suddenly moved, and in its place it's like, *"What am I supposed to sit on? Where is the energy?"* And in comes Love. *"I am Love. That is what I am made of!"* We allow Love all through our being, and after a while, the whole body goes, *"That is brilliant!"*

Some time later the whole body goes, *"Ow! I really am in pain!"* And you stop and you say, *"What's going on? The pain is where the old emotional pain used to be, which is getting my attention. Love is there, but it is not actually making a big enough impact to let my body know it is Love."*

You then work on getting across – *"I am Love"* – and gradually the body goes, *"Oh! I can relax now."* The body starts to get better and better, and then you discover you have done a complete circle.

You changed the energy by changing the negative thought! You apologised, worked that through, and let it go. You didn't need that energy, it's negative. You let *that* go. You find you need more energy and fast, and all your tissues are getting better, and you get that in, and then you understand that what you just put in is love! And it is what you really are. And the body loves it!

When you begin to realise that you have been born at this most important time in history, what are you doing about time? About essence? How are you helping? Your *Spirit* has the whole programme figured out. You don't have to go out searching, it will come to you. But please change your way you are thinking about you, if you can.

Remind yourself:
- *I am the leader of my group.*
- *I am the leader.*
- *I am whole.*
- *I am beautiful.*

It is not saying, *"I look beautiful* or *"wonderful."* That is ego. The soul and the essence are the truth, and it is easy to forget that *"This is me and I don't have to pretend it."* This becomes important in relationships.

"Do I love him as much as I love me?" is your next question to you as you are evolving, and you meet up with someone. Your first thought is, *"I love the feeling. I love the sense of being part of."*

In a lot of cases people go to a *belonging*. They are *belonging* or *feel complete*. We forget initially that we are already complete.

How many times do you hear people say, "I am going to ask my other half?" Coming from the place of *"I am love,"* the whole of you moves around completely aware of what she loves and doesn't love in life, where she gives and takes, and where she will not put others before herself. She is downloading her standard of self.

What is so vitally important with her is that she is in every equation that is going on and saying, *"I matter! I am down here on behalf of my Spirit"* And if there's something negative, like for example: *"I am not down here to be bullied by you! I am very willing to meet you halfway in this, or whatever feels comfortable,"* – you feel it – *"but I am not being told by somebody else how to run my life."*

How do they take that? If they come back to you with something hurtful, how do you handle that? Ask yourself, *"What am I doing?"* or *"What am I not doing?"* that is stopping what is coming my way. It is the ability to be able to say, *"That is my job. I am not expecting, and I don't want you to own me, because you can't."*

Erica: I feel like I have done so much work around this, and I always feel like I do love myself, but then there must be something in me that is still holding on to that belief, because I have this pattern – but I am working on it – where I have nearly achieved something that I wanted, like teaching Pilates, but then I start getting this pain in my arm which slows me down. I injured myself twice when I was trying to do my teacher training because I wanted to teach Pilates. It is like there is something that is making me self-sabotage and I am aware of it. I have been trying to do work around conscious connected breath to release whatever there is.

Denny: Have you asked yourself the question, *Why?* One of the greatest things that *Spirit* does is that they will muck up your career if you are on the wrong one, as far as *Spirit* is concerned. I was an opera singer. It was my life. I loved being on stage. And then my voice gave up because my intercostal muscles were so damaged, I couldn't sing. I had to give up my life of opera which was all I was ever, ever going to do.

You can only find your truth by a feel. It is not a thought. You cannot do it by thinking because you get an ego answer. So, your life is reflecting back to you. Who are the players going to be? What kind of players are you going to have? There might be lovely players. There might be players with a rough edge, and you ask, 'Why? Why do I recognise that part of me that I don't like? When have I first met this age before?' And if you are good with a camera inside your head, you can put yourself up for a meditation, and then ask for the age you were when you first felt that emotion of applying unkindness, unfairness, whatever it was to yourself.

Whoever you get to be, the only person you are actually out to impress, is you. Please do the best for you that pleases you. And feel good about what you have done. That goes out in your energy field and is felt by every single person observing. Consciously, they don't know, but they will be picking the essence up unconsciously. And that is a key point in anything you are doing – you are only doing it for you.

Erica: Everything you said was going on in me. I just want to say thank you and I'm just sending you so much love and appreciation for having this call with me. I am so glad that it happened and that it was meant to be. I wanted to feel that connection with *Spirit*. I know that I always have that connection, but I sometimes think I am blocking it by doubting, worrying, and trying to control things. But the "100-Days Ancient Secrets" course and this conversation with you reminds me that God is with me all the time.

Denny: Yes, all the time. And certainly, so is everyone else's. My love for you! Well done! Know that you are important! Particularly now!

"The essence of Love is beautiful beyond words. And when living within Love, there can't be any negative thoughts. It is quite extraordinary."

"We only have one Master.
We only have one person we have to
answer to, and that is our Spirit,
our essence, nobody else."

Session #10: Ben

Acknowledge, Praise, Thank, & Love Yourself.
Don't Fight!

Denny: We are just going to let our essences join and enter into a peaceful moment and then we'll see where we go from there.

Okay. We have here a very beautiful soul, but insecure. The soul is not insecure, but the beloved ego is doing all it can to try and make the essence insecure. Somewhere along the line you are looking to how you are seen and how people see you.

You seem to have forgotten that the only person that is important here is you, as the essence. Before you ever came back, your essence chose the journey and when we are pure essence, there is no ego. Not having any physical awareness, that means not feeling discomfort here, we bravely say yes, and back we come having totally forgotten the intent and any suggestion initially that the essence is part of us.

The journey is all about coming back to the essence, coming back to the truth. It can take hundreds of lifetimes, or it can take ten. At the moment, it is your lifetime today, and was your last lifetime and the lifetime before, coming towards this wonderful awareness that you are essence. You are love. But your beloved ego is having quite a battle.

Some of that is a trauma, and the upset and shock of someone passing because it was so unexpected, and you were so unready. That trauma is still sitting within you, and you are keeping yourself incredibly busy, so you don't have to face it yet, which is absolutely okay. Well done! It is your defense mechanism, and

211

we are seeing this wonderful growth in such a short time as you have taken on huge responsibilities.

Since then, you are having a bit of fun on your own and I am looking here at the brilliance of what you are achieving in this very, very short time, which is quite extraordinary. Your achievements have only just started and yet they are quite outstanding with what you have already achieved. Yet in and amongst all this, what are you searching for? What is it that you are hoping to achieve from it for you?

Standing beside you is a young boy aged about four. It is you and you are looking very concerned. Can you go back and meet up with you at age four, and see what it is that you are looking at? Can you see yourself at age four? Who are you with?

Ben: The image I have is with my mom. I am really shy. Someone comes to the door and I kind of hide behind her. I don't track any particular event; I just know I was really shy and didn't like to talk with strangers.

Denny: There is something in the four-year-old that is the first concrete foundation of a thought form that is still with you today. If you look at shyness, it is also the difficulty to speak. Did you have trouble speaking?

Ben: I just didn't want to talk to strangers. But I would talk a lot if it was my family or friends. I wasn't old enough for school, so it was before kindergarten, or anything like that. We moved when I was four. I think that was the age when we moved.

Denny: Well, he is up beside you today, so he is in on this session. Obviously, he needs to hear whatever it is we talk about or find to reassure him that he is heard. He speaks beautifully. He has a natural flow of language and the fear of being seen is getting easier and easier. Being seen is a form of responsibility to you and it is a mantle you are not too sure about taking on. I think you would have preferred to wait about another five maybe ten years before you were asked whether you would like to take the mantle on.

You weren't asked at all; you were just landed because your essence knew exactly what it was doing. It was your humanness that didn't, and it is your humanness that is still in shock. It is our ability to go to the ego part of us and say, *"You are beautiful, you are wonderful, hang in there, we had a shock, but this was set up before we ever came back. This is part of my journey, my learning, my offering to the world. My Spirit guides me, and I have gradually been trying to understand the difference between ego and Spirit."*

The better you are at moving towards being and understanding this beautiful word 'love,' and understanding the joy that comes with true love, the more apprehensive, at this moment, you become. Why?

What is the voice within your beloved ego that is trying very hard to make life tough for *Spirit* at the moment? It is like ego is making a desperate fight to hold on to its position, knowing it is getting weaker and weaker, because you are understanding love more and more.

Just feel this beautiful being. Feel it right through your body but understand it is not up against the edge of your body, it hasn't got that magnificent freedom to soar out, unless we leave the body for a while. We have been asked by *Spirit* to do this journey and within this energetic structure are carried all our fears, our emotions – predominantly negative – but in it there is fun and laughter.

So often we move away from love and joy because that is too easy. We've got to make life hard. We have to undo so many of the traps and tribulations that come from growing up in whichever country, in whichever religion, in whichever world we are growing up in, to fit certain patterns, to fit certain behaviours of what is acceptable and what is not acceptable. And whilst all this learning is going on we have no say, so often no explanation, and yet there is such a fountain of love around you spreading around the world. You are having to learn how to embrace it.

When I asked you to feel you, can you tell me what you feel?

Ben: I feel this light. It's not real pain in the body. It is transmitted into the body. It's beautiful light.

Denny: Do you own it? Do you know that that really is you? The whole of your energy field has gone into reverse. It has gone, *"No, I don't think so, Den."* I don't think it is ready to do that yet. It wants to. What are you frightened of?

Ben: Nothing, even that light, or the 'me' that is light. What is it frightened of? Are you asking what is my essence afraid of?

Denny: Not your essence, your ego.

Ben: Oh, my ego.

Denny: You are embracing your essence. You are doing absolutely what the essence is asking of you.

Ben: Hmm, ego is afraid of being forgotten, marginalized, extinguished, being unseen, not knowing. Let's see what else.

Denny: Okay, so who does ego think it is doing this for?

Ben: The ego feels it is survival for existence.

Denny: We only have one Master. We only have one person we have to answer to, and that is our *Spirit,* our essence, nobody else. Not how the world sees us, not how others see us, not whether we have their approval or disapproval. It is of absolutely no consequence.

We are answering to our essence through total truth. We are respectful of self at all times. We honour and obey what truth is always asking of us and we are able to tell the difference between ego and truth because ego will always have a negative connotation to it. Truth has nothing except love.

What are you asking from everybody else?

Ben: You are asking me what am I asking from everyone else?

Denny: Yes

Ben: To love more and trust more in *Spirit.*

Denny: In real life, what is it that you are looking for?

Ben: What am I looking for? To be loved, feel loved, feel safe, feel useful, and that what I am doing is meaningful. Those are the things. And to enjoy the moments.

Denny: What I am looking at is a part of you that is worried it's not going to get the recognition, which is your ego, for what it is that you are doing and the work that you are doing. I think what I keep picking up is that you don't register that you are the essence that was asked for by essence. I think you feel that there are better models around and you do a comparison, instead of, *"I am this essence being born absolutely as I am meant to be. I am forgetting that I am it all in my own right, but I keep looking out and doing a comparison with others. I can't do what somebody else can do."*

It has got nothing to do with anybody. It has got to do with what your essence asked of you, and it is absolutely to do with the love you have and this incredible ability you have to bring together these wonderful facilities, people, groups, that can expand. And yet, you do not say, *"Well done,"* enough to your-self. No ego yearning, there is nothing arrogant or cocky at all. This is absolute love. *"I am meant to be like this. So why am I so worried about it?"*

Are you aware that you are having trouble owning your own essence as being absolutely what it is meant to be?

Ben: So, what you are feeling is that there is some kind of a struggle in me to accept myself as the perfect expression of the essence, of what I am here to do and to be, which is perfectly me. Instead, I am looking outward and saying, *"Oh, this person can do things I can't do,"* or *"Others can do stuff I can't do."* And I am not accepting my perfection of me being exactly who I am, exactly right now, in the ways in which I am doing it?"

Denny: Absolutely perfect! But you are also ignoring the mag-nificence of what you are now. You are not owning the essence of you now. You are still drawing comparisons instead of being able to go, *"I am working 100% with my essence. I am it all."*

Every one of us is. We could save the world. We could do phenomenal things. But when we 'go home' that isn't the issue.

The essence wants to know what have we achieved in that line of learning, in that school of life? Have we achieved and overcome in our ability to love all that we are? Have we moved beyond the need to assess ourselves with others? Have we grown beyond the need to change that behaviour so that this person finds it alright?

Am I able to own my own essence, however wobbly I feel, and follow truth in such a way that nothing can change where I am coming from, as long as it is coming from my truth?

Your truth will always be completely neutral, whereas, if the ego is involved, you will always get a sense of being not so comfortable. In comes the doubt voice, *"Should I, shouldn't I?"* Whenever that comes in, you stop what you are doing straight-away and connect to your essence. *"I am what I am meant to be! Why am I trying to muck it up? Which part of me in my growth, my journey so far in this life, has gotten in the way?"*

Bit by bit we gradually learn.

Your little four-year-old has come in again. It is very interesting. He is concerned about being there. Therefore, his shyness is still an active part of your behaviour patterns today, I think, without a doubt, although you rise above him. I don't think he is being heard by you enough to understand how shy he really was and how much he hurts with the shyness in him. He is far too sensitive, and I don't think his future, which is you, has really appreciated what this boy has done. How he has held on, how he has held him, and he is still there. He is still inside you and he still isn't sure. We need you telling him how wonderful he is, how magnificent he is, how proud of him you are.

I have worked quite a bit with children, in all the areas, and the amount of, "Well done!", the amount of praise, the amount of connection is so important. And yet how much do you do to the youngsters that are inside of you today?

Our children from birth, they don't disappear. They sit within us. When I first learned how to meet my yesterday children, I ended up with, as you can imagine, quite a few. I built a special place in my imagination where we could all meet, from the tiny baby in the cot to much older.

When I first built it, I used to go down and they all used to rush and clamp on to me and there was great love. They were wanted. They were loved.

We are both sitting here now – we haven't gone through what they have – our inner children have done all that for us. So, to really look at this again and just see how beautiful these inner children are and what they have managed to go through in learning for me, and how they survived, how they have handled it, I will look back and say, *"Wasn't that magnificent? Wasn't I magnificent?"* They need to hear that.

My essence knows, my ego knows, my ego can quieten down now. It doesn't need the negative. It is beginning to see how wonderful I have been all the way through with all these lessons put for me to use and work with.

The ego gets less and less, and you become safer and safer with all of you that makes the whole. You feel their love and you feel their joy, and you feel their acceptance of you because you have accepted them. You love them for what they have managed to do for you. That is the foundation which grows bigger and bigger and bigger. When you go out into this world with the great gifts that you have got and your next chapter emerges, you have this powerhouse of pure love standing behind you, which is you. You are answering to your essence, nothing else, and you will always know by the feel, not by the thought.

You are a great 'head' person. As you can get more into the heart, you will get better and better. You have a very, very clever brain and it wants to join in and make things fit together, which leads to getting stressed very easily. This is why your four-year-old is here – a very stressed little four-year-old – so shy, stressed out of his mind with shyness. He is still with you today. He is still that shyness and that part of him is very well hidden by you. He is still there, and he is the only age standing by you. The others aren't, not yet. He is very strongly there and that is what this is. It is this part of you that is very frightened to let go and be all that you really are because you haven't done it yet.

This shyness creates the *"What if? Am I acceptable?"*

You are acceptable to the world but only if you are acceptable to you.

The world simply mirrors us. I learned so much from that learning but remember that essence is only interested in your growth, what you are achieving, and the lessons that were handed to you. Can you move beyond them or are you going to go under with them?

And like a stubborn Denny, I will not go under. It is love of self, not an undermining of self. Not the comparison of, *"I am not like him"* and, *"I am not like her,"* and, *"I am not this."*

If you were meant to have been any of them you would have been, but you are meant to be Ben with very, very big reasons and you are showing those reasons bit by bit, but you are taking fright because your shyness is still there, and we haven't addressed it yet.

So, we are going to need a lot of loving of our little four-year-old, five-year-old, and the other ages that might come up. We are going to bear witness to how little time you have given them, how little love and appreciation.

You simply say, *"I am sorry it has taken me so long to get back to you, but I am here, and I love you, and I am your future and look what you have already done for me. You are fantastic, and I am so proud of every single one of you."*

Bit by bit those little ones are going to start turning towards you and going, *"He does care, he does understand! He knows how hard I worked. He knows how shy I was, and he hears me."* Soon you will have all those children on board. As I said, mine lived in a very special fantasy world filled with little trees and little houses.

Our essence is looking at what we are doing with the learnings that we were all sent back to study, what we've done for the world or, *"Do people like me?"* or *"Will they remember me?"*

You are there half the time, coming from a place of love, and then you slip back into the old ego with all these fears and worries coming up. For example: "Am I getting it right?"

Remember, it is a feeling. Does it feel right? "Yes, okay, I can do it. I can check and I can listen to what is in my heart, which tells me the truth." And if any part of your heart is doubtful then don't listen until you find out what the doubtful bit is.

Your whole system is asking for time out to honour these children, as they have been forgotten about. It isn't just Ben today. It is all of what made Ben what he is today that is so beautiful – but he needs to know that, and own it, and understand it. There is no ego. It is our love for what we are. We are essence, far more than we are ego. We are doing the work and journey on behalf of essence. How does that fit your thought patterns today?

Ben: I understand that we are far more essence than we are ego. You said that at least half of the time I am there, and then half the time I am in ego. There is the possibility to honour each part of me, each age of me that contributed to who I am. And the one that is standing closest to me right now is the four-year-old boy who still hasn't fully been seen or acknowledged or appreciated, and so is still laying on that shyness and not wanting to be seen.

Denny: It is very important to hear what they want from us, not what we think we can do for them.

Ben: So, listening to him? Asking him what does he want me to feel? What does he want me to see or understand.

Denny: Yes, and just get the feel of them all. This is the beauty of you as they all make you. They make this wonderful being. Remind yourself: *"I am it all. I am every age that I am."* And that makes you so wonderful – when you know them, when you understand them, when you honour them, and give them the love that maybe they haven't had so much of. *"I am it all."*

I love you.

"We cannot give to the outside world what we can't give to ourselves."

Session #11: Carol

Love & Other Wonderful Gifts That Help Us with Our Learnings
Receiving Answers and Truth

Denny: Welcome, lovely to meet you, and I am all yours. I am connecting to your energy fields while we are just becoming acquainted and matching energies. Why do you think we have come together today?

Carol: I kind of fell in love with you the first time I saw you, and Clare as well. What a beautiful daughter you have. What a magnificent *Spirit* that she has as well. So beautiful! I have been intuitive most of my life. *Spirit* gives me information to help people, usually total strangers, but I am unable to help myself, or my children in any way. Well, that is not entirely true. I have been able to help myself because I have been a lot better this year than I was before I started the 'Ancient Secrets' journey.

Denny: When I saw you, I saw a shadow line and that shadow line to me is family ancestral clearance. It is as if what you have been birthed into is part of your journey in clearing, as much as we can, but you are not doing it alone. I am trying to work out which one is still with you. At the moment it's you that I am looking at, and I am a bit concerned about the shadow part. It's as if you haven't been aware that it is there. Do you know it's there? Are you aware?

223

Carol: I am aware of it much of the time. I have incredible guides that have a wonderful sense of humour and they even take me on a journey to unknown places. I was a stranger in Canada, and they said, *"You need to get out of that hotel room and go get on that bus, go to the corner and make a left and then go right."* I ended up in a bookstore in Canada with a rare gem of a book that changed my life. They have a great sense of humour. There is that, and there is darkness.

I went through a really dark time of having out of body experiences and feeling I was being consumed in blackness and falling out of control. I saw a Spiritual psychologist who helped me to get through that phase where I would say, *"In the name of Christ, you must leave. If you are not for my good, you must leave."*

Denny: Oh well done! I have a phrase, *"Please show me that you come from the light and your light is brighter than mine."* You repeat this three times, and the third time, they cannot by cosmic law, they cannot stay if their light is less. Every student of mine is taught that right from the beginning. I am delighted to hear you say that! You are the first person that I have heard that is already doing it. Absolutely brilliant.

When we leave the body, we actually go through the biggest traffic jam, which is where *Spirits* who have just died are, and some of them are not going to move any further at all. Some of them are drug addicts, or *Spirits* looking for a fix, an alcoholic fix, and they are trolling, literally just above. You go through that to get to your essence. But if there are any vital signs of control, we demand to be shown that it comes from light. This is not taught enough. It is so lovely to hear it from you, it really is.

But I do think you are very much involved in the ancestral and it is coming up time and time again. Every time I am starting on another subject, it is coming back. You have not covered ancestral healing enough. It comes from the women's side because it is the womb each time. You are carrying your mother's life, and she is carrying her mother's life. The egg is there. It is bearing the history, but in your case, we have tools. I am being told that tools are in place for you to help clear some of the weight of what's going on.

I can see water has something to do with it. It has to do with an ancestor way back who showed great disrespect to water, and each subsequent person involved in this particular journey of learning carries this symbol of water. Water can cleanse, it can help sort you out. I feel it's arrogance. We humans are so good at arrogance. It's like we need to turn the key that opens and unlocks the door of love because it doesn't flow out naturally at times.

But let's come back to you because I am getting a lot of that through your daughter, but this is about you. Let's talk about you.

Carol: I retired in May of last year and I am volunteering for the Ancient Secrets Foundation and helping to put together trainings. I was mentoring before, but I don't know what my future holds. My skill sets are really good for what was needed – I do data analytics, and spreadsheets, and analysis, and I do a lot of genealogy and I have had some brilliant connections. It is really interesting – the journey. I have studied just about everything there is to study as far as religion and healing. I was working on a PhD in natural health, but the school went bankrupt. I thought I would be in New Mexico working as a naturopath, but that door closed.

Denny: That is ego, full of ideas of what it could do.

But you can say, *"Thank you very much, I'll actually find out where I am going when I get there."* Try to teach the ego to stop directing you and for you to try to stop feeling that this has to be the way.

You are on this planet and the vibration has gone up. I don't know how many vibrations, but over the last six years scientists are measuring the planet again, and as Earth rises up, the vibration of the earth is going to have a direct effect on every single one of us, be it animal, plant, or anything that has life. Everything is being affected by Earth's vibration. One of our difficulties is our body needs to get used to these vibrations, which are high, and we can't escape them because we are on the planet, and if the planet is going up, then we are going up, too.

But the adjustment is harder this time because it is a big movement, and it is our ability to say, *"Okay, this is different, but it is far more important. It is not going to be the same, I am not going to know where I am going, I am not going to be led. It is going to come to me, and I am just going to continue to do everything that I am happy to be doing."* Out of it, *Spirit* will tell you, *"This is where we want you to work."*

You don't have to worry about what you are going to do. Your *Spirit* has been training you all this time, for exactly what is coming. Your job now is to illustrate your learnings by seeing how important each one has been, and how it is interwoven into your present life – what you are still tidying up, what you are bringing together, what you are saying goodbye to. And that is very important as well. We are saying goodbye to a lot that does not fit the new vibration and your beloved essence is making damn sure that you remove what is not necessary. It doesn't want any of us to carry wasteful stuff that is no longer of value to us. There are a lot of us who are going around like, *"Thank you very much, but no thank you, ego, I have discovered really what Spirit is all about."*

The most important thing is, at the level that you are, it is coming to you. It is your understanding that you are here on behalf of your *Spirit*, and to be aware that your beloved ego, which we all have, will be trying to say, *"But I didn't tell you you'd be doing that.*" Ego gets very upset if we follow the essence and it is not involved. And ego's great delight is telling you why it was wrong or why it was right. It could be the opposite of whatever you decided to do.

It is our ability to say, *"Thank you, but no thank you. I thank you for all you have done, but now you are no longer relevant to where I am. But thank you so much for being relevant all this time."* It is letting ego know how much you do appreciate it, but letting ego know that *ego is not essence.*

What I have found myself doing is teaching my students the art of being able to tell through their body *"Yes, this is correct,"* and, *"No, this is not correct".* When it is your truth, it is your essence that speaks to you. From your neck downwards, your body can only speak truth. From your neck upwards, your ego is involved.

There are ways of teaching 'yes' and 'no' because truth, when we speak it, has no emotion. Truth is truth. If it has an emotion, it is called ego. If it has got anger or an upset, if it has passion, if it has any emotion at all – good, bad – it is never going to be truth. This is very maddening for ego, because ego depends upon emotion.

What I have been teaching everybody is to learn your 'yes' and 'no' response. Do you know how to recognise the 'yes' and 'no' inside of you?

Carol: I probably do not.

Denny: You can check if you do. Sitting up or standing, comfortably straight, relaxed, you are going to say to yourself: "My name is Carol," and what you are looking for is a sensation in your body. That inclination to go forwards? That is a 'yes.' If the body goes backwards, that is a 'no' response. Let's try it.

Carol: My name is Carol.

Denny: Any movements?

Carol: My name is Carol. It definitely feels like it is a forward.

Denny: Alright, next test. My name is Jemima Puddleduck.

Carol: My name is Jemima Puddleduck. Definitely feels backwards.

Denny: Now that was done simply because your body knows the truth, and there was no argument. Ego didn't have time to come up with an objection. I didn't ask you a question that was of any importance to me so there wasn't a muddle. Do you have a question that has got a question mark to it now, that you don't know the outcome yet that we could share?

Carol: Will I be able to travel? I want to go to the UK. I want to go to Italy. I want to go to Portugal.

Denny: Just have the question. Just ask your body.

Carol: Will I be able to travel within the next year to Europe? I am getting kind of a side-to-side instead of a front-and-back.

Denny: Yes, that wasn't a very safe answer at all. In two years?

Carol: Will I be able to travel to Europe within two years?

Denny: There is a strange block. If I want to, can I travel Europe next year?

Carol: Okay. If I want to, if I desire to, will I be able to travel to Europe within the next year? I am getting more of a forward sense on that one.

Denny: Yes, that is better but there is a block there somewhere, something to do with freedom. Like you are not free to travel or the arrangements you'd have to make would be very severe, but there is space. One of the things you need to look at is the tendency to get into your own way.

You start thinking on behalf of others when you are in that equation. Therefore, instead of being equal, you are putting yourself down here. That does not serve you because:

> *We cannot give to the outside world what we can't give to ourselves.*

Basically, you first must put your own backyard right and understand your own backyard, which takes a lifetime; well, I am sure my last breath will be, *"Oh gosh, that was that!"*; I'll still be learning. It is a school of life. It is the journey of learning and finding it becomes easier and easier because you have realised that love overrides everything.

Carol: Love with understanding?

Denny: Love with understanding, to a certain extent. You don't have to understand. Last week, I had probably the worst week I have had for a very long time with physical pain, and I got to a point where I didn't know what the point of living was really all about. I was so distressed with the amount of pain, and I suddenly got a flash through my head, which was *Spirit* going, *"Love."*

And I replied back, *"It doesn't matter whether you love or not. There is just too much pain, and it doesn't seem to ease, however much you love, or whatever else goes on."*

And back came, *"Love just is. What are you?"*

And it quieted me straight down. It made me stop and look at how many other thoughts I had put into this misery of pain and couldn't cope. I was full of, *"It is not fair. I have had this for so long."*

It was so wonderful the way love just went, *"We are still here."* We can't change anything, we can just love. If you just pay attention to love and not all these other words coming out, you'll understand the power of love.

This is probably the greatest gift I have ever been given – to really register love.

Here is an example that has been so useful in my teaching:

Years ago, I had a landscaping company and I worked with so-called 'naughty' children, 16 to 18 year old 'criminals.' You have never seen such miserable children. I just wanted to adopt every child and bring them home and give them some love and show them what a parent was. I had 12 boys and 12 girls, 24 all together, and we had a marvellous time, we had such a successful time, but that really wasn't the point.

The point was, in their developing, nobody had given a damn about them. The parents were the ones that failed them. They, the parents, saw them as losers and they, the children, were just desperate. They stole from clotheslines or would beat somebody up – various things like that – but nobody had ever been looking at what had gone on before in their lives and discovered the hurdles these youngsters had gone through. It was lack of love that was shown to me, because nothing that anybody taught these youngsters made any difference to their lives at all.

One day I was working in the office and suddenly a flash came across my mind, *"Create football matches."* I thought, *"Football matches?"* *"Yes, football matches,"* my crowd answered.

So, I got a group of six staff and said, "We are going to have football matches and we are going to see who we can play." We did our research and found we had sixteen teams we could play against, and they all said, "Yes, that it was a great idea." I supplied the footballs, the shirts and organised everything. My only rule in my organisation was that every single person had to play. It didn't matter for how long, but the organisation was the team. I didn't just want somebody to play football, I wanted everybody who represented the team to be on the team.

The fortnight before the match, some of the boys were walking past me, looking at a wall – basically anywhere but me – and mumbling. I said, "Are you talking to a wall or are you talking to me or what?"

One of the youngsters asked, "Are you going to the match?"

"Yes, of course I am going to the match," I replied. "Of course, I am. I am going to watch you lot. Can you play football?"

The youngster replied, "Yeah, but will you be watching me?"

"Of course, I will. Why do you think I'd be going down there if I can't see what you are all doing."

"Ugh," he mumbled.

And off they went. This went on over the fortnight with the girls and the boys. They couldn't look me in the face yet because they didn't trust a single person, but they all understood that I would be at the match watching them. I got my staff together and I said, "We all need to make notes and write down everything we see happening out on the field during the match, and we'll meet afterwards and make sure we have written down something about every single child."

On Monday, we were back at work, and the children were all there and we had won. We were all there carrying on and nothing had been said. Then I walked past one of them and I said, "I thought you were supposed to kick the ball and not fresh air."

He just curled with laughter, and said, "You saw?"

"I saw you kicking, and you missed the ball all together," I said. "I thought you were supposed to kick the ball!"

He choked up with laughter and said, "You are! I missed it!"

Those were his opening words to a grown-up: laughter. It was the first time that they felt the love that not one of these youngsters had received before.

We took part in all six matches, and won them all, and they were presented with a cup that I'd spent the money getting. We did it all. We broke the ice with love.

These youngsters, they knew. I had seen that these were young criminals here, but I knew why. On one occasion I dared to go in and say, "At the back of the hangar there is a car, and in that car was a case with very important insulin injections. Somebody has stolen it. And somebody has stolen it from my crowd here, and I am not impressed with any of you. But I am going to go back to my office, and I want that case back by that car now."

And it was. Just like that. I never asked who. I never asked anything.

They started to trust. The emotion behind it was a terror to be loved. They wouldn't ask and that is where the depth of love started to grow in me phenomenally. It was such a powerful tool. It didn't matter how grumpy or difficult they were, they couldn't get past the love and somebody caring.

This is your line, Carol. You are very much involved in this. It is finding the key. I found mine completely by accident. There was a collective action which showed that every single person in our group – my group of criminals – was receptive.

The key starts with love and what I am saying very firmly to you is don't go looking. Carry on the work you are doing, and it will come to you because *Spirit* has trained you the way it wants you trained, and you have gone with it very beautifully.

You have been hurt; you have been injured. You still have wounds. I can see them but then you are owning them. They are not owning you, if that makes sense. You can work to clear some of those to lighten you more, in the sense that there is more of your light shining and more of the shadows just gone and not needed, so you are more free for the work that *Spirit* is asking you to do. But I need you to stop searching. Realise that you are getting closer and closer to where *Spirit* wants you to be, and you are doing it brilliantly.

Carol: Thank you. I do try to clear anything that I have picked up energetically that is not serving me. To detach and to recover my own energy, like emotions, that I have given away and left with others. To gather to myself all that I need to sustain myself energetically. I do those visualisations and meditations to bring in my own, and to detach that which doesn't serve me.

Denny: Very good. One of the things that the *Spirits* are talking to me about is exactly what you are saying, but they are putting it slightly differently. You grew up thinking you wouldn't be heard very well; that you weren't a very important person.

Carol: Lacking self-esteem, yes.

Denny: Perfect! You've got it in one. It has taken you a very long time, and it is still around that part of you that forgets that she is the one speaking on behalf of her *Spirit*, not on behalf of her ego. When you are trying to bring you back, you are doing that on behalf of *Spirit*, not on behalf of ego. That becomes so important to understand, that you are doing it for your essence and that you are essence.

I have worked with *Spirit* guides that have come from different planets and because I am psychic, I obviously travel a lot – and think you do, too – but you end up in different places and you realise life is not the way we know it. It is still life, but it is often more intelligent than we are, and you must accept that or be willing to let ego go and not assume we are the only or most important planet.

Let's focus on why we have been born *now*, with this amount of learning behind us *now*. What is so important for us to be here now? It is this enormous change coming which has already started. Do you feel that?

Carol: What I feel is that vibration has become so much more evident and important. I knew that in the corporate world I could come in with positivity and raise the level in the room. I could support someone who was floundering with their words and boost them up energetically so that their words became clearer, and their message became clearer. I never drew attention to myself. I was always in the background, but I was doing a great deal of energy work there. That becomes more and more evident: how our vibration can affect others and how we are able to raise that level if we are mindful.

Denny: Yes, yes! You see how much you are being used now by *Spirit*. You see how different it is to how you were.

That is something to take note of, sweetheart, because it is a new you emerging. And it is a new path emerging. And all you are going to be doing is new, but from a very old soul.

So, it is going to flow. You are not sitting there going, *"Two and two make four."* You have got it all. You are miles ahead. You are on this next chapter, bringing into this brand-new world and vibration. With the next phase you have all the knowledge you need, all the tools you need.

It is lovely to watch your energy dancing while we are talking. It is getting caught up and it is getting very interesting. It becomes calm and peaceful, but it needs to trust itself more. It needs to trust its feel. Especially using the "yes or no" tool. So, when you are going to make a decision about something, you do the "yes or no," and you go with the first answer because the second answer is going to be ego.

We have a marvelous example:

Gill and I both did a 30-day detox. Well, I didn't. I did two to three weeks. Gill did it all. We were out, and we both looked at what we used to love, and said, *"Oh yes, we'll have a slice of cake. We'll eat something illegal just this time."* Both of us could hear the voice inside, the voice of the truth, going, *"No. No."* And both of us went, *"Well one slice is not going to harm anybody. Yes, please, we want it!"* We were both ill that night and it was an absolute example of how we got a *'no'* and we took a *'yes.'*

Carol: Willfulness.

Denny: Total. And we are all still doing that. Be aware but be very loving when you are putting it right. What Gill and I both said was, *"We are so sorry, me, I have done it again. But well done, me, because I have seen it, and I'll remember it quicker next time."* Each time we thank ourselves for seeing it, the body says, *"Okay, we heard,"* instead of being really cross with ourselves. No, it is pure love. It is so simple. It's our relationship with who we are that counts.

If anything shadowy turns up, settle down, and ask to be shown why that came into your life and *Spirit* will show you. Then you can work it out. But again, you do it with huge love. Maybe you have to leave it for some time while you are just being there, but it is love.

It is so hard to get this across: it is your love for you as essence that changes our world. You are getting closer and closer and closer to that. It is beautiful to see it in your field. You still have got one or two patches to go, but who hasn't?

Carol: I saw a little sign on a shop wall that changed my self-esteem. It said, "God doesn't make junk." And at that moment I had this epiphany that I am not really junk at all. I am really something God made that has worth.

Denny: Oh that is fantastic, absolutely fantastic. Yes! So, you have an interesting life, sweetheart! You are going to be led more and more in what you are doing. You have got ancestral life with the women down your line. It is clearing while you are not aware of it. You are all right at the moment, but it will come. So, you tell me, what have you gained?

Carol: I think time with you is so precious. I have looked so forward to this because your *Spirit* exudes love more than any I have ever seen. Just to be in your presence, even though it is over electronics, is so moving because your heart is so pure, and your motives are so pure, and it is so rare. I am so grateful to have this time in your presence, so thank you.

Denny: I am very, very honoured. I hope we meet again.

Carol: I hope I get to hug you one of these days when I am in Europe.

∞

Carol reflected on her session with Denny in January 2022

The session with Denny had an enormous impact on my awareness of the voice of my ego. Realising after the session with Denny that much of my decision-making during my long high-tech career was, in fact, ego driven, was a real eye opener. Why worry about what tomorrow may or may not bring, when *Spirit* so artfully prepares us for whatever is coming!

*"Remember we are the project,
not what we do."*

Session #12: Elissa

You Are the Common Denominator,
You Are the Project &
You Are the Most Important.

Gill: Elissa was diagnosed with an extremely painful neurological disorder called, Stiff Person Syndrome. Denny felt they were very similar and had to experience their life learnings through body pain.

Denny: I need to know more about the condition you have called, 'Stiff Person Syndrome.'

Elissa: SPS is a neurological disorder. It causes your muscles to spasm so violently that they break bones, dislocate joints, or tear muscles and tear ligaments.

Denny: Now that I know, what I want to know is, what is it like having it?

Elissa: Hell.

Denny: Yes. Any respite anywhere?

Elissa: Yeah. I was in a hospice for two years, and one of my hospice nurses decided to change my 80 milligrams of Valium a day to eight milligrams of another medication, and I stopped having attacks every day.

I got on that medication, which got me kicked out of the Hospice, and now I am on palliative care because no other doctor wants to write prescriptions for doses that high, even though when I was trying to stay with the doctors I had, I was able to get down to four milligrams a day. But if I go below that, I start having symptoms.

That is the only place in Texas where I can get the dosages of medicine that I need, and the muscle relaxer, which is the only one that works for me. Texas is talking about prohibiting it because so many people have died taking it. I know people that died taking it. They went out drinking one night, came home, took a couple of these muscle relaxers, and never woke up again.

I take different medications *and* this muscle relaxer, so I know just simply having one drink could push me over the edge, where I'd stop breathing and wouldn't recover.

I also have a condition called orthostatic hypotension, which means my blood pressure doesn't adjust when I stand up.

Denny: Yes, low blood pressure. Oh, I have that, and can be standing talking one minute and the next minute I am being peeled off the floor.

Elissa: Yeah, it's frustrating. It's frustrating as hell! One time I had gotten up, taken a few steps, blacked out, had a seizure, and at some point during the seizure, it became very clear to me that I didn't have to stick around and deal with this. I had a choice to leave my body, and not have to deal with the pain and being a burden to my family, and those kinds of things.

Denny: This is very, very similar to my story.

Elissa: When I was lying on the floor, I really thought about it, and decided I couldn't do that to my family.

Denny: I've had similar experiences. Three times I have had the wish to go home because of the pain and three times I was told, *"No, you haven't finished the work you have got to do,"* which I think was extremely unkind of *Spirit.*

Sometimes I argue a lot with my *Spirit*, but we love each other greatly, and it took me a long time to realise it wasn't my choice and wasn't my time. When you are like me and you – when you are in a lot of pain, and you are having a bad day with pain – the last thing you want is to be of any use to anybody or to help someone. You are in survival mode, and survival mode is getting the very short end of the straw. But I know life is vital, it's where we learn everything.

Elissa: Apparently, I *chose* this path.

Denny: Yes, exactly the same as me. The question is how can we love ourselves when our body is struggling? For example, I can hardly walk, I can't do this, I can't do that. So therefore, why am I useful? Why am I doing anything? How do I enjoy life?

I have got the most magnificent friend and carer in Gill, who you met earlier, who does all my knobs and buttons and various things for me. But it took me a long time to realise that I couldn't just decide to 'go home,' regardless of the pain.

Elissa: I have had a couple of people who told me that it was okay for me to say, "Yes." My mother and brothers say they would be okay, but I don't believe they would.

Denny: Your beloved ego would say, *"Oh, yes, fine, off you go,"* which is what my ego tried to do. But your *Spirit*, what you and I really are – the essence of what we are – the reason that we have been sent back into this human form is to go through the learning we've said we would go through. And as far as I am concerned, everybody's got to have a look at this blueprint before we decide we are ever coming back.

Elissa: Yes, I want to say to *Spirit*, *"I am a good person. I have helped other people. Why? Why do you want to torture me like this?"*

Denny: It does not matter what we do for others, it only matters what we are doing for ourselves. *We* are the project, not what we *do*. It's what we are towards ourselves, and that's something that's very important to try and remember!

Most people put others ahead of themselves, which is the most destructive thing one can do. One has to say, *"I am doing this for love of me. Every action we take is a learning. Every pain we feel is a learning. Every bit of joy that comes into our lives is a wonderful bit of learning. Every time we smile, laugh, it's lovely learning. It's our essence. It's our soul.*

It's not my body's fault. It's the experience that my essence wanted me to go through, even though I didn't ask for it, but we need to be able to say, *"Thank you."*

I am still able to catch myself making a really unfair comment about a part of my body which is screaming nightmares at me today. I say, *"I am so sorry."* And then I go on and say, *"But well done, me!"* because I have seen that I am doing it. In my apology to that part of my body, that part of my body relaxes and knows it's being cared about, and that is making an incredible difference to the whole of my body. I do all my learning through my physical body.

We need to look at our own areas of discomfort and understand that our respect for who we are is because we are essence in a human body. We are not human bodies having a Spiritual experience. We are the other way around. We are *Spirits* having a human experience. The human is the only energetic structure that feels, nothing else feels.

> **Gill:** When Elissa was a young woman she served in the Navy where she got pregnant but lost the baby and never stopped grieving and was depressed for many, many years. Denny noticed that Elissa's energy field was bouncing in very bright yellow.

Denny: You try to bury your feelings by being busy doing head work. Your body hurts instead of the thought. If we could change some of the thinking to eradicate pain, that would help a lot, but it would mean that you would have to be prepared at some stage to say, *"Okay, I am sick of this particular pain. I need to go deeper and find out where the hell it's coming from, and I need to clear that. I am the captain, and I am ready to clear it.* We can clear it because *Spirit's* timetable is always in the now.

A tremendous amount of past lives can be changed/healed, but you have to get permission from *Spirit* to change those lives because they affect other people's lives as well. If *Spirit* says "Yes," we can go back into a past life and pick out the trauma.

Let me give you an example:
One of my clients came with severe asthma and we went into a past life where we discovered she had been a really harsh, unkind, male captain of the ship who bullied the crew. The crew disliked him intensely and at some stage they mutinied. And in

the mutiny, they tied the captain to a plank and threw him to the sea as a punishment and took over the ship.

My client, in her past life, a) didn't want to die, and b) wanted to correct his appalling actions. We asked *Spirit* for permission to put things right because this was going to affect those who had been part and parcel of that experience – those other players. Back came the answer, *"Yes!"*

My client (the captain in her past life) ended up on a kind of raft, being pulled back in by the sailors. He was apologising most profusely for how horrible, how ghastly, he had been, and saying that he would do every shift on the ship to show that he *did* know how to captain.

My client had permission to do this, which meant that all the crew that had been involved in the killing of the captain also got forgiven automatically by his actions of putting it right.

When we finished the whole thing, she sat up and said, "I can breathe!" The asthma was gone, and she never had asthma again!

The asthma was the water lapping in her mouth, where she couldn't breathe. By her forgiving herself she healed her own asthma. (I did nothing. I just was able to support her through the story by her own desire to put it right.) Now that is how powerful our essences are!

> **Gill:** Elissa expressed her worry for her brother who is also of ill health and, having cared for her dad who was very ill for a long time, she was concerned that her brother might end up the same. She became a Reiki master to be able to help herself and others heal.

Denny: If you are a healer, you know perfectly well, we can *offer*. They don't have to accept, and we do not personalise it if they do not choose to receive. We have done our best. If they want to ignore, that is their right, and the consequences of their actions are theirs. It's their life, not yours.

You are the essence. You are your project. Your brother has his own *Spirit* and his own project, as does your mother, and your other brother. They are not attached. They all are *Spirits*. Remember that we are all on our journeys, and the ego can get in the way as we know and make a mess of something, but it's not your job to lie in bed and cry. That's a complete waste of your essence.

If your brother is not learning in time, that is okay. You can still love him and honour him for his efforts. They are not your efforts. You are not him. If you were meant to be him, you would have been him. So don't cry, because you have to love yourself, and you are the only one that matters.

The healing and learning to heal is more for you, because you are the project, not what you can do for others. You've got to do for you first. I learned the hard way. Until I could sort out my own backyard, as I call it, with all the horrible things that have gone on in my life – until I was prepared to look at that, feel the pain of that, and work through it myself – I couldn't help the world.

Remember we are the project, not what we do.

More respect please, from you to you! We need to understand that your being is what is so important. Nothing about what you are doing. Your actual being alive is all that matters as far as *Spirit* is concerned because that is what you are, and you are the project. If your *Spirit* wants you to do something, your *Spirit* will show you.

Let it come to you and allow your beloved body to get used to how it is. I have to get used to pain in my arms and legs and it's like, some days it's hell and other days it's semi-hell. Other days it's not too bad. Other days it's really quite variable. There is still pain, but it's not my body's fault. There is no blame game anywhere. There is only love and love just cancels everything out. It's really quite comic when you get there.

One of my biggest steps of growing was when I looked at a whole lot of past issues, where I hurt. I was very into the blame game: *their* fault – particularly the orphanage – and it was a gradual realisation that there was one common denominator in each of these stories. Different players, but one common denominator, and that common denominator was me. This meant that every player there was there on behalf of me.

They were there teaching me some lesson that *Spirit* had set up. They were like teachers in university, one way or the other. Once I realised I was the common denominator, I had to stop the blame game. You can't blame anybody when they are there on your behalf, so the blame game stops. You can't blame yourself either because your own *Spirit* set it up. So as a blame game goes out, in comes love.

Hear me when I say you are the common denominator, therefore it's happening to you for a reason, and it's our ability to look and see why. *"Why was that there for me? What was I learning from all of that?"*

You can't blame anybody. You can try but what's the point? You are not going anywhere with it when you've got the hate and the fury and the rage. I can't blame or accuse anybody, and I certainly can't accuse myself. I just might as well let it all go and see what's left, and bit by bit (and it was bit by bit because there was an awful lot of rage, anger, and pain in me), but the gradual realisation that they were there on my behalf, because I was the only common denominator and these people weren't in other scenarios further on, that I slowly began to realise that – *It's a play!*

We must have done something very interesting in one or two of our lives for *Spirit* to decide that now is the time to have these particular learnings. We are still here, so we must be doing something right.

But you need loving. The love I am talking about is a big one that says, "loving myself and remembering, I am love, that's what Spirit is." This is how we are made. Can you remember that?

Elissa: Yes!

> **Gill:** Elissa lives with her mother and would like to move out to be on her own but is not sure whether she can do it because of her physical condition.

Denny: Don't put it as a definite. You are scared now. It's difficult for me to work it out, *yet*. You know, *yet*. "I haven't got a handle on it, *yet*."

That gives you all that time to work it out and you've got a *yet* when your essence hears and goes, *"She is determined to do it, we will help."* So, you've got that *yet*.

I want you to listen to every sentence you make and if it's a statement with a negative, you put *yet* on it, and instantly change it to positive. If you make an unkind comment about yourself, start off by saying, *"I am so sorry, me. I have just heard what I have said, and I have been most unfair to you. Thank you, me."*

Always thank yourself when you recognise, and you'll do less and less, but your language needs to change, sweetheart.

*" 'Should, could and ought' –
these words are all banned with
my students."*

Session #13: Francesca
Let Your Body Guide You & Trust

Denny: Let's just tune in together. Let me have a gentle wander around your energy field if it's okay with you. I see all sorts of interesting things. That *is* interesting. Your energy field, your aura, do you know what I mean by energy field and aura?

Francesca: Yes, I do.

Denny: It's becoming deeper in colour. It has been quite pastel. Have you been ill?

Francesca: Yes. yes.

Denny: Seriously ill?

Francesca: Yes, I had cancer.

Denny: Yeah. I am seeing the shape of it. Looking at your body, the colour is becoming brighter. Which means the body is recovering. It is recovering and rebuilding. It has gone from pastel shades to deeper shades coming in. What I say to that is, "Well done!" You can see where it was, and you can see it is not there now. So, we are now paying attention so it cannot come back.

Okay. Your energy field is saying that it is winning the battle. You are winning. You are doing well. Your body has changed a lot, I can see it wasn't that long ago.

Francesca: No, not really, it has been nearly four years – three and a half to four years.

Denny: It had to be a fairly bad one for me to see that your energy is still becoming richer. It took a lot out of you. But I like what I see there.

Francesca: You know, I have to say, sometimes I'm worried and thinking, "Am I winning this battle?"

Denny: That is a thought form you want to remove. The other day, Gill and I were having a deep discussion concerning some clients and the government with their new laws coming in to do with COVID and vaccinations. Everything is built on fear. The latest is you need a confirmation on your mobile to say you have been vaccinated or you are exempt. If you haven't got vaccinated, it's being said you won't be allowed to attend certain places or travel. You are being blackmailed slowly based on fear.

COVID is not in my reality. I don't see it. A tremendous amount of my work is taking that fear factor out. We were talking about the fact that we are going to have to go against our truth, with *Spirit*'s understanding. So, this is not our truth that we are having to honour the human element. If it wants to do anything, it wants to go anywhere, it is going to have to obey these new laws.

The part that worries, "I could catch it, I could get cancer, it will come back," *you* are putting those thoughts in. That is what I call "an imaginary box" that floats between us and our true *Spirit*, although we are *Spirit*. But we send off these ideas without realising what kind of ideas they are.

Francesca: Well, actually, I must say that I am debating with myself if I can be off medication for cancer completely, because I hate this medication. It creates all kinds of side effects, you know. It stops the menstruation cycle, and everything else. And I have been debating with myself if I am ready to stop taking them, because I can see that my body is getting better. But, of course, it can never be a natural balance if I continue taking this medication of an injection every month.

I realise that sometimes it is creating an internal conflict because there are these different voices. There is one part of me that is ready. I can trust myself not to be here again. Okay, so I know that I have a voice and that voice is quite a strong voice. But then there is also the other voice of fear with, *"You can continue taking this medication for another year or something. Let's wait until the protocol is over."* So, I'm in this struggle a little bit.

Denny: You are absolutely right. The thing to understand is truth is another word for essence. Our truth is our essence, and we feel it. We don't think it, we feel it. The feeling is from the neck downwards, it is really in the solar plexus and the guts. It is where *Spirit*, our essence, can actually speak its truth.

I do nothing without checking. I have been doing this for so many years now that I just live by my feeling, not by my head. Sometimes we think we are running our lives, we forget that actually this was all chosen for us by our beloved *Spirit*, our essence, for us to explore the emotional aspects of everything we have gone through.

We have coped the best we can. We coped brilliantly, from an ego place, because that is where we have all been coming from, how we've all been taught.

For example, we might compare ourselves with another person, how they look or what they wear. We then start to have these 'wonderful' words from parents and teachers, *"You should have done that! You could be doing this! You ought to be here!"*

Should, could and ought – these words are all banned with my students.

The other word we have to work with is *pride*.

For example, when we are trying to impress others. I have never understood the need for this. We are all on our journey, and none of us knows what our journey is. We might have similar pains, but our stories are different. They are fitting what our essence wanted us to experience. Our essence chose when you were to be born, whom to be born to, and chose an extraordinary time in history to be actively busy now.

You are right at the age where you are vital in a generation of waking the world up to Spirituality, our climate, and more. You have all the training and capabilities you came in with. Whether you are using them, I don't know. You have had to experience cancer to take you to a level of fear, pain, depression, and powerlessness. But then your strength and fight came in. You needed those learnings, which have given you the tools that you have from surviving your cancer and becoming what you are today.

This is fascinating to see you use with others. There is a part of you that is going, *"But it is me. What can I possibly teach anybody?"*

You are the project. Are you aware of that? You don't have to do or be something to be a project. You and your humanness are the project. You are back here, trapped in the human body, unable to get out and be free, like our essence, to do the journey on behalf of our *Spirit* in order to have the emotional pain and emotional learning that we said we would have a go at. What you have succeeded in doing so far is so much growth through your own personal pain, it makes sense that you can see pain and cancer in others.

The first time I saw MS *(multiple sclerosis)* just with my eyes, I saw this looked like a water bubble on this woman's head. All I could do was watch it and look at it and it seemed to move. But I had no idea what I was looking at, except I knew we had a problem. Little did I know that I was actually looking at the start of MS, but I learned by what I saw.

I never diagnose. I wouldn't be allowed to by my guides. I always say, "I'd like you to have a check-up with the doctor just to prove that everything's okay." That means, as far as I am concerned, I can't find anything anywhere.

If I can *see*, I'll say, "I would like you to fix a date with a doctor as soon as you can, which would help me to know what's going on." That is the closest I can get. I don't put a name to anything unless that person knows they have already got it, if that makes sense.

One of the biggest reasons for that is love. If you are healing, and repairing, I am seeing this wonderful healing energy going through someone. But worrying about it could bring it back. It stands out like a sore thumb and is a thought form going on that is of no use to anyone, only a hindrance.

Francesca: May I ask you something? Before I had cancer – I had two surgeries on my back. One was for a slipped disk and my body has been going through chronic pain for so many years.

Denny: I know many people including myself, that are learning through pain in our bodies.

Francesca: Yes, yes. A lot of pain.

Denny: Yes, lots of pain, and I would like to do it differently. Because, at the moment, I am very limited in my movement.

Francesca: There is one doubt I always had. It was kind of an idea that I was always full of fear to go and live my life. Somehow all this pain, especially my back pain, caused me to need to lie down.

I am wondering if all these blocks that my body creates are because I am not ready. I never feel ready to live my life. It sounds like I am still waiting to be ready to fit into my life. I think even cancer has been kind of like this.

I was not surprised to get cancer. I was 37 at the time. I always thought there was something wrong. I thought, *"Well, it is cancer, so let's see if I survive it."*

Now I am on the other side and feel like I'm in a kind of different transition.

Now I can see that I can heal. And watching this process of healing I've been on – it's been an incredible year since I started – I can see my body has recovered and changed shape completely. But at the same time now I am thinking, *"What do I do now?"*

Pain has been part of my body for so long. Now I don't know what to do with myself. You talk about this project, what do you mean?

Denny: I hear you. What would it be like if you suddenly walked minus pain? Knowing you are safe, knowing your back was okay, knowing the cancer has gone, and 100% healed? You are as perfect as you were when you were born, and you will be just as perfect the day you die. It is the bits in between where the ego lives, in the body.

Now, it is the body that does most of your talking. It's where the ego sits and is the lowest form of our intelligence, but it does its best for us. But we give it far too much power and our ego always works with a negative emotion. *"I worry about getting cancer."* This is all negative.

You are the project. Not what you do. We are so good at pushing ourselves down the list. Everybody else is more important than we are. You decided you are going to get there, but at the moment you are forgetting you are the project.

I had an experience many, many years ago now, probably 15 to 20 years ago.

I found myself bidding farewell to a wonderful client. She'd rung me up out of the blue. To cut a long story short, she had been working with me for five or six years, and everything had worked well. But she'd fallen into this magnificent ego trap. It was one of those situations where I could see, but couldn't do anything about it, which is what makes it so sad.

My client had ovarian cancer, which we were working well with, and she had a friend, who told her that there was a fabulous cure for ovarian cancer in Austria. The operation cost £6000. She said, "It is exactly what you need and it's going to cure you." My client said, "Well, I don't have £6000. Thank you very much, but no thank you."

When she came for her session, we discussed it all, and she was able to talk to her own *Spirit*. I teach all my crowd to talk to that part of them. They need to connect with their truth. Working with *Spirit* teaches them their truth, giving them answers. Plus, it teaches them when *ego* is giving them the answer. We had our session and her higher self, her *Spirit*, very loudly and very clearly said, *"No!"* She listened, and she had her answer.

But I got a phone call about three weeks later and she said to me, "I've killed myself. I am dying." I said, "What are you doing, what's going on?" She replied that her husband, who was a big part of the whole learning curve of the journey, had found the money and paid for her to get the cure, and in her eyes, it was a lovely gesture. But she went for the treatment, and after it, she knew straight away, thinking of what *Spirit* had said, she had gone against her truth.

I saw her three times after that. I went every other day because she was so ill. She went from being okay to dying fast. She asked a favour of me: to drive her to the nearest garden centre where she could bid farewell to all the plants. Gardening was her passion. I had to drive at almost no miles an hour because she was so delicate. She had morphine jabs attached to her. I put covers around her and love around the car. I did everything I could to make her comfortable. We got there, we did it, and took the journey back.

Once back, I helped her onto her bed. She wanted to connect to her higher self, which she saw as a white horse. In the past when she connected, she was never allowed to ride her horse, only stroke it. But while she was connected, she suddenly said, "Denny, I am being put onto the horse!" and she was lifted up and put on the horse.

From being this frightened, terrified lady knowing she had killed herself, she called out, "I can see where I am going, it's wonderful! It's all right, it doesn't matter. I can sit up here now and go home."

I said, "That's absolutely fabulous! Let's wrap you up and snug you down. Your daughter is going to be here any minute now. I'll go. Everything's okay and I'll see you in two days."

I kissed her goodbye, came out and got in the car to drive home. But I thought, "No, I'm not ready to go home."

I really didn't know where or who I was. I drove into the nearest town and parked the car, got out, and was looking down at a lot of people walking and children running. But all I could see were people rushing madly to do things. Doing, doing, doing without thought. I just couldn't take it and couldn't understand what was going on. I got back in the car and drove until I found a country lane where I parked. I wept like I have never wept. I wept and wept.

Eventually, I was Denny again, but what had happened? I had moved with my client's energy to where *she was*, which was halfway between 'going home' and being here on the planet, if that makes sense. But I was in my humanness. I wasn't floating.

I was witnessing humans missing life after life after life after life, because we were letting ego run our lives. We take the ego as the truth, not our essence. The learning of this now became so vital for me to be able to continue this kind of work, because I was more than just with them, I knew where we were going. But at the same time, I realised I could only love them on their way and love them as I held them while they did the work. Phenomenal!

The next day I received a phone call to say she'd 'gone home.' I knew she'd gone home on the horse.

Two days later, I am sitting at home on the sofa reading and listening to music. I had a lovely little dolphin, which my client had given to me, and suddenly it flew from the mantelpiece, onto my lap, where I was reading! Of course, I realised it was my client getting my attention. She had come all the way back to say, *"I am home, it is wonderful, no pain and I'm okay."*

This is where I learned how important our time down on the planet is.

I have been in a very tough patch this last week with so much pain, like you talk about with your back. My body won't work properly, and I have had to hold on to the thought, *"It is okay, I can handle it. I am love."* I have been on a detox, which I think is getting towards the end, for which I am going to be eternally grateful. If it wasn't for Gill, I think I would have given up, but Gill has supported and encouraged me regardless. I couldn't do anything without her help, and the whole of it stems from love. There is no blame game for my body. *"Why have I got this?* Or *"Why is my body doing that?* Or *"Why does my heart misbehave? Why? Why? Why?"* That is ego.

Our truth sets it up. It wants us to experience what it is like and move beyond the need of it. That is exciting.

Right early on you made a marvelous statement. *"What do I do if I don't have pain?"* Instead of, *"Look at everything I can do, when I don't have it!"*

You are a free person. You are in a body that doesn't hurt, that isn't ill. It allows you phenomenal freedom, which you don't have at the moment because you don't know what your body's going to do next. So, you could say you are running away from success. Except you already know success. So which part of you wants to hold on to the fear? The *"What happens if I am ill?"*

Francesca: Well, I think my desire to move further in my life is there. I can feel it. I always wanted it. You know, I never gave up on myself. I always had that light. *"Let's move further. Let's go ahead."* But at the same time, I was always terrified of my own destiny, if that makes sense. I survived the surgeries. I made a difficult decision and refused chemotherapy, and I am still here. I checked on my medication and I am still here. I test myself a lot. I think I test because I need to know my powers. I test the power, so to speak. I don't know how to explain. It is an ego thing, right?

Denny: Yes, reminding you that your *Spirit* knows you have got every gift. You were sent back with every gift. It depends how long we take to find the gift you have. Also, so often it is to face them. We are much better at facing failure or tackling failure than we are with success.

Francesca: Yeah, that is exactly the point, I think.

Denny: You are at a very important time in your life, age-wise, experience-wise, love-wise, everything-wise. The only thing that puts everything right is love. Nothing can hit love. Nothing can destroy love. You can destroy different types of love. We come back to ego. Human relationships can get damaged, they can get pushed. The love we are talking about is the essence, which is love.

So, every time we have a negative inside us, it is the negative ego. The essence, your truth, has nothing to do with it because all the negative emotions belong to ego. Our beloved ego battles through. Battle is so often a good word, it shows courage.

Years ago, I was talking to someone about our elements. I remember saying I have never found the fire element within me. Back came the response, "You are full of fire energy. You can't see it because it is being used to help you with your illness." All my fire is in survival.

Francesca: Yes, I can see that, actually.

Denny: Right. I could not. I never saw it and it was a realisation that I was looking at so many of us indirectly, including myself. I had to try and understand more of the wonderment of humans because when we are having a tough time, as you know, it doesn't feel wonderful or magnificent. Definitely not. No, it can feel bad, lonely, and isolated. It feels good having loving people around you, but it is still you suffering. It has to be you first. Because if we are not at the top of our love list then we cannot love anybody. Your *Spirit* is love. That is why the magnificent healing comes through.

So, getting back to you: What are you frightened of? Responsibility?

Francesca: Yes, but I don't know why.

Denny: When you are doing something, you can only be responsible for yourself. Love is such a powerful tool. Love changes all of that.

You are living your life and there is suddenly a difficult person. Your reaction is, *"I am not going to play this game. I am not interested in a fight, and I don't want any of this."* As they come towards you, you say, *"I am gonna lift my vibration higher. I am just loving up here. I am just love, nothing else, and you just go love, love, love, love, love,"* and you don't stay on their path.

You have moved and they stay on that path looking for what you were. They see you, then they lose you because they can't find that energy to have a fight with, because it's up here. The difficult person carries on, unable to find you. It is simply that.

Francesca: Oh, it is so interesting. Because that is what they did when I was diagnosed with cancer. That was my conversation. I said, *"Thank you very much, I get it. But now I need to ask you to leave."* I trust that conversation more than everything else.

Denny: You are absolutely spot on right. We are quite remarkable how love can heal. How love can stall out pain, trauma, agony, what we carry, what we are going to meet. You know how to love, to keep that one going, and be away from anything that is trying to harm.

Francesca: Yeah, I am just thinking that maybe I need to go through a few days of retreat or something, because I think my head is just confused. Because I am not listening too much, or maybe I am just overly, you know, just stressed or tired. And that is what maybe, what has been missing – that I don't know what to do with myself because I am not listening carefully. So, I am just a little bit all over the place. I get different emotions through a roller coaster of emotion every day because I, I just cannot find a balance in this.

Denny: Don't worry about it, but understand, at the moment, right across the planet, the whole of the planet has raised its vibration. Because the planet's gone up, everything living on the planet has gone up, too. So, every living thing is on this higher planet, and none of us have been there before. We all said, "We'll do it, we'll cover the ground. We will be the transition, and the next generation will take it on to the next stage." But the body needs to get used to it, and in so many cases the body is having difficulty because stuff is coming up to be cleared out.

The COVID problem is bringing a lot of our shadow up in the form of loneliness and anger. It is spreading itself all around the energy field. When we go out, we can walk into the energy, so it can affect any one of us. It is affecting us, particularly the old version of us. But *Spirit* is dropping the old version of us because it doesn't need it. It is not relevant to this new vibration and so we have to let go. We have no escape on this planet. Where this planet goes, we go too.

You are here to understand. There is a tremendous amount of

work we can do together to maybe change some of your thinking, because that is the thing to love. Coming at it from a loving perspective as opposed to being aggressive or upset towards self. To understand that our body is doing the best it can for us.

Let's also remember that the woman sitting opposite me today didn't go through the cancer, the back operations, or the other injuries and damage that have been done to you. It didn't happen to *you*. And my life didn't happen to *me*, the woman sitting on the sofa looking at you. I am carrying the ages that it happened to, and they are the ones that need the love and the healing.

Same with you. It is not you *today*. You didn't have experiences, and we are very good at imagining that we did. "This happened to me. This was done to me." No. "It happened to me *then* and I can love that *me* of yesterday better."

> *Be far more gentle with yourself.*

You are very beautiful and lovely, but you back off too much. You have a lot to offer, and you are not seeing it, or you don't want to see it. It has to do with responsibility, but you won't be doing it alone. I don't do any of this alone because I always get my *Spirit* guides with *Spirit*. They are the ones I talk to. They give me the subject and steer me.

Is my truth coming through to your truth? Can my *Spirit* attach to your *Spirit*?

Francesca: Yes, totally.

Denny: Excellent.

Francesca reflected on her session with Denny
December 2021

Francesca: I chose to have a session with Denny as a birthday gift to myself. It was my 41st birthday. Italy was going through a long lock-down period. I felt quite lonely, and to keep me light and busy during the weekend, I was studying for the "100-Days Course in Ancient Healing," thanks to a scholarship provided by Dr. Clint G. Rogers from the Ancient Secrets Foundation.

I was impressed by Denny and her wisdom since day one, seeing her on the "100-Days" course calls. I spent a decade in the UK, and I loved listening to her British accent during the calls. I was fascinated by her communication style, which I found so unusual for a British lady of her generation. Especially being so open about the sexual abuses and violence she experienced. She was owning her story while talking to complete strangers in a way which was truly unique and inspiring. She sounded wise and sweet, but confident and assertive at the same time. A rock made of love, ready to help us find our lost souls.

That is how I saw her. There were no traces of the horror she had experienced in her facial expressions. Her age marks were soft, just like the tone of her voice. She reminded me of some Buddhist monks I met. She was emanating light, spiritual strength, and peace.

I wanted some of that power and listened very carefully when she was speaking because I wanted to capture her secrets. How she had managed to transcend all the pain she had been through.

I was struggling with the experience of chronic pain, cancer, and loneliness. I was doing my best, but certainly I wasn't feeling like a good embodiment of peaceful wisdom.

I got really excited when the possibility of talking to her in a one-on-one session was offered. I chose to help Gen with the organisation of this book as part of my volunteering work and the community. A book on Denny's life and wisdom was something I definitely wanted to contribute to.

I wanted to know more about Denny and her incredible life journey, so I prepared a list of questions for Gill to pose to her, to learn more about her life, ideas, and perspectives. Above all, I really hoped that Denny's teaching could help me deal with my own pain, to unlock some of the blocks that I felt in my life and help me find a way forward. It was a lot to ask, I know, but it is the truth.

When we first started our session, she noticed that I had been seriously ill in the past. Her psychic capabilities were full on. I don't look like a woman who had cancer. I have long thick hair, wide shoulders. I am very tall. Most people, including doctors, need to take a double look at me, before realising that I am a person with an impressive medical record. It took Denny five seconds on Zoom to see what was going with me. This is how remarkable a person she was and how acute her perceptive skills were.

In the months that followed her transition, one single sentence from our session that I found myself coming back to over and over again was: "*You are the project.*"

What she meant by that is I am the real project in my life, the only one that really matters, not the working, creative, professional projects that I was busying myself with and identifying as my life's mission at the time.

I repeat these words to myself like a mantra. This helps me stay focused and be more gentle with myself, to find balance when I am feeling overwhelmed or guilty for not working enough.

I tend to be very self-critical and have the tendency to feel inadequate and not successful enough compared to others. This was another point Denny touched on, reminding myself that it is all about my journey. This was an important message that she delivered so powerfully and yet so simply.

I read the transcripts of our meeting multiple times and I am surprised each time by the accuracy of her perception. She figured me out so easily.

I know that she was channeling most of her words and she was right. The fear of getting ill again and of feeling pain. Physical pain is a major part of my suffering, but the real game changer was the exercise that she gave me. The exercise she suggested doing was relatively easy: to ask my body from the neck down for decisions that regard my health. I was quite dubious at first, but it turned out to be a lifesaver.

The first realisation I had while doing this exercise was very scary. After our session I started practicing this exercise of asking my body and observing whether it would shift forward or backwards. I was not very confident about my ability to understand my body's answers at first, so I decided to practice it after one full day of silence and meditation that I was doing for the "100-Days course in Ancient Healing." One of the burning questions for me at the time was deciding whether to continue on the same protocol for breast cancer patients or to quit.

I asked my body what to do and listened from the neck down, just like Denny suggested. The way in which my body responded was shocking.

My body was moving like a different force was guiding it forward or backward. I felt like I was hallucinating! My perceptions were higher, perhaps because of the full day spent in meditation, and were unmistakable and surprising.

There were clear indications to stop taking all the medications. I was contemplating quitting for a while, but I never considered stopping all medications together. I didn't follow this advice immediately. I didn't feel ready or confident enough.

After a few days, perhaps a week, I had a terrible blood pressure surge. I got so ill that I had to be taken to hospital for a night, and from that point onwards it was hell. My blood pressure was out of control, going up and down. I consulted different doctors, did all kinds of tests, but no diagnosis was made, except that my body was having a bad reaction to the medications I was taking.

This was my hypothesis, and it was supported by some of the doctors, but all were prudent in suggesting I quit medications completely.

I was very ill and weak. I could hardly work or even walk because my blood pressure was so out of control that it posed great risks to my health. Doctors didn't know what else to do and a new oncologist tried to replace the old medications with new ones, but the new drug produced severe side effects right away.

Everyone was puzzled. At that point, after two months of struggles, I understood that listening to my body was the only option, and luckily, after quitting all medications, my health slowly improved.

The coincidence of me not listening to what my body had clearly suggested after my session with Denny and the terrible consequences that followed was quite obvious.

I learned to follow my body's indications the hard way. Sadly, Denny transitioned while I was still trying to recover from the blood pressure surges. Therefore, I didn't have a second session with her. I continue to do the exercise of asking my body what to do religiously. I do it all the time now, even when I am shopping or when I feel tired and don't know whether to cancel or postpone an appointment. It has become a new daily routine. I check with my body before taking a painkiller. I pay attention to it, it is like having a new line of communication, which is not based on thoughts, but on the body.

I was able to re-establish a direct line of communication with my body, thanks to Denny. I listen to my body, or at least I ask my body every day to help me figure out the correct way of living.

I have done many therapies in my life but none of them was as effective and left such a deep mark in my consciousness after a single session. Denny's teaching stays alive with me and guides me through using my body every day. I still regret canceling my second session because I was feeling ill, but having this book helps me to identify the steps forward that Denny would have suggested. I can find many inspiring lines in other people's sessions as well as Denny's life itself.

I can only say, "Thank you, Denny, and your *Spirit*, for showing up in my life. Thanks to the Ancient Secrets Community for being the platform that allows us to meet, and thanks to my own *Spirit* for allowing this learning."

I consider it a real blessing to have crossed paths with Denny. Her vision, the way she saw and lived life and *Spirit* as one, and her belief that even the hardest lessons are what *Spirit* wants us to learn from is a continuing and humbling inspiration for me and I believe for us all.

"Every one of us is on our own personal journey."

"The journey that one is being asked to remember is very simply that everything is love."

PART THREE

An Incredible Journey

"In my journey, I have discovered an unbelievable number of difficulties can still exist in our lives, but there are wonderful tools to help overcome them."

CHAPTER 4

Tools For Life

Who Am I? What Am I? Why Am I?

There are so many different avenues to find out who you are or how to find your path. Working with these three important questions sets my clients on a path to opening themselves up and suddenly seeing within them how beautiful they really are.

Question one: *Who am I?*

You are actually *Spirit* sent back in human form to live life on this planet. Some people think it's the other way around, but I like to say:

> *You are not a human being having a spiritual experience.*
> *You are a spiritual being having a human experience.*

Question two: *What am I?*

You are the project. Not what you do or what you achieve. Not what you can do for others. You've got to do for you first. You are it all. You are the whole project.

Question three: *Why am I?*

We are sent back into human form to learn through emotional learning and understand why we have that emotional learning, and what we need to change. Every action we take is a learning. Every pain we feel is a learning. Every bit of joy that comes into our lives is a wonderful bit of learning. Every time we smile, laugh, it's a lovely learning. It's our essence. It's our soul.

> *We start off as a chrysalis and*
> *we end up as a butterfly.*

Love Yourself First

This is your journey. Yours alone. The first thing you must do on your journey is to learn to love yourself. Slip away the concerns of what you look like – physically and mentally – or what people think of you or how you want to be represented. Understand you are everything you are meant to be. You are perfect at birth. You are perfect at death. And you are perfect in the middle. *You are Spirit. And Spirit is just love.*

> *On a really, really bad day,*
> *when I am having difficulty communicating,*
> *and I'm in bed going to sleep,*
> *I will often just say quietly to myself,*
> *"Love, love, love, love, love, love,"*
> *and 9 times out of 10 it will settle me down.*

You Are Not Alone

I know we are made up of love and we are never ever alone, so we can feel total despair but never ever think we are standing separate. We can't. We are each other and we are there to support each other.

Call out. Yell. Anything you need.
Somebody will be there.
Something will occur.

You will then realise that you are being heard. It could be through a book, or meeting a friend or a stranger. It could be crying about something and releasing tears. But let it come slowly.

Remember, even when you are at your deepest despair, you are never alone because you have *you* with you. Your Spirit never leaves you. And there is always another chapter ready to happen, waiting for you.

Listen to Your Truth

Sometimes when clients come to me, they might be in a bit of a tough patch and could be having a really hard time physically, emotionally and/or spiritually and are not sure what to do. The one thing I always say is, "If you are not sure what to do, just be in the truth. Be in its simplicity. Be in its acceptance of you. Trust yourself and be in your truth."

The Pendulum Test

To be in your truth, I teach all my students to learn their 'yes' and 'no' response, using their body as a pendulum. In this exercise I am asking you to pay attention and be respectful to you. Sitting up or standing – comfortably straight and relaxed – you are going to ask yourself a question. What you are looking for is a sensation in your body. That inclination to go forwards? That is a 'yes.' If the body goes backwards, that is a 'no' response. Let's try it.

- Sit or stand.
- Close your eyes and go to your meditation space, thinking of your question.
- Feel the truth.
- Advice, ideas – let them float around.
- Take no action and speak no words that do not respect you.
- Ask yourself your question.
- If your body leans forward, that is a yes.
- If your body goes backwards, that is a no.
- Because your truth has said no, your truth will make you uncomfortable.
- If your truth has said yes, you will feel good.
- Listen to your truth.

Choice

One of the tools we have is very tied up in understanding that *we actually have a choice in how we think*.

It's extraordinary how many people don't understand that you can choose to change your thoughts. You can change feelings of anger, despair, and basically all sorts of negative painful feelings. We don't have to hold on to them and let them run our lives. We can change them.

An example:

In recent weeks I went from being perfectly okay to having a massive nosebleed. I have had the occasional nosebleed and it always sorted itself out. But this started and I paid no attention but then it got worse. I called for my beloved Gill and said, "Help!" I told her, "We got a real problem here!" We couldn't stop it, it just poured and poured and poured. Eventually, Gill connected with the ambulance service. The paramedics came and they were absolutely lovely. They saw and could see the damage and very low blood pressure. I really was basically a mess and I was pouring a lot of blood and Gill had already changed my clothes once. But I kept on having very large blood clots, too. So, I had to go to a hospital.

The first hospital put me in the corridor of A & E, where I stayed for hours. No doctor saw me. I was then transferred to another hospital. Again, I was left in a corridor on a stretcher, which my body was really struggling with. My body was hurting! I hadn't had any medication, water, or anything and I still had the nosebleed. I was then left for another 3 hours at least, because it was now nighttime. Nobody came and asked if I was okay, or needed a drink, or anything. I was not happy.

But then I suddenly registered that every thought I was having was negative: How *awful* the corridor was. How *terrible* the nurses were. How *unhelpful* everybody was. *I was just a number.* Right in the middle of thinking all those thoughts, I thought, *"What are you doing Denny? Every thought is negative! Why should anybody be wanting to help you? You need to change your whole attitude!"*

So, in the corridor of this hospital, I sat and did the exercise that we all can do, which is *change where I was coming from.* Change my thought patterns and attitude.

The doctors and nurses were trying to do their job and doing their best.

I started to send out lots and lots of love, thanking every-body with my love. I kept going, and it must have been within half an hour, one of my doctors arrived back. I was weeping at that point with the sheer pain I was in. But I was still sending love.

The doctor said, "Den, we can't have this! Have you eaten?" I said "No, I haven't eaten nor had a drink since nine o'clock the morning before."

He literally disappeared and came back with an egg sandwich and a cup of coffee and proceeded to sit on the side of the bed while I drank and ate what I could of the sandwich. Then, he said, "I am coming back. I will be back!" He went chasing, and apparently let fly amongst the medical staff, about my physical condition, where I was, and the state I was in. Within half an hour, I was moved to a cubicle, which had its own loo and basin. And even sorted out a special mattress, plus I was given my phone and kindle from my bag.

So, from changing my anger and feeling very sorry for myself to sending out love and apologies for being so selfish, my world changed. This is a good example of what happens when we change our attitude and how we feel.

The Golden Circle

One of the best tools that I have used over the years for sorting your feelings and letting go, has never failed to assist. I recommended it in several of my sessions in this book, but it's always good to review this exercise. I call it "The Golden Circle."

Before you do this exercise make sure you are not wearing jewelry.

- In your mind, create a lovely golden circle of energy on the ground in front of you. It's like a paddling pool and the sides swell up and you see it growing, high enough so it can contain its contents.

- When you are satisfied with level of the sides, take a deep breath and step into this circle.
- The first thing you do is drop every negative thought in your body into the golden circle. You just drop it. Strip the negative thoughts down your body as if you are getting ready to change into your swimming gear. You just let it go.
- Once you have dropped everything that needs emptying, I want you to step out of the circle and face it. You are standing outside, looking into the circle. It is holding a whole load of your negative stuff.
- It is full of other people's negativity as well, which was getting in the way of you.
- You take a step back and take note. *Are you still feeling exactly the same?*
- You continue stepping backwards until you sense, *"I am not feeling this anger, this anguish, this difficulty, this pain."*
- *"I have left it in the pool, in the circle. I am watching it. I am in control of it, but I am walking my body out of those emotions."*
- You are only dropping negative thoughts that were running through your body and are not relevant anymore. Anything good stays automatically.
- The next thing to ask yourself is, *"Am I feeling (not thinking but feeling) that I want to go nearer to the circle?* Because you are coming from a non-emotional place now, you may feel you'd like to take out a theme from that paddling pool and debate and discuss with it.
- You are now coming from, *"I can see you and I am in charge, and I will decide what I want to do with you in the end, if anything."*

- However, if you suddenly think, *"I don't want to do this anymore,"* you don't do it anymore. Your body is not ready.
- It is okay to leave all the things you don't need *in* the circle. You don't have to deal with them or take them on board again.
- You can leave your golden circle alone now, but every now and then check it.

LOVE is the only emotion needed in the world.

Staying on the Right Path

There are many different reasons for having difficulty in this life. Ask yourself what is upsetting you that is causing you to have difficulty. Are you unhappy? Depressed? Angry? Upset? Is somebody harming you? Do you feel safe with who you are? The reasons are going to create behavioral patterns. It is the act of very lovingly, gently learning how to take ownership of who you are that can help you understand yourself and see how beautiful you are.

- Try to gradually change your behaviour towards yourself, one step at a time.
- When you start respecting yourself, others automatically respect you. Because you only do to others what you do to yourself.

- If you harm yourself (physically, emotionally, mentally), you'll harm others.
- If you have sympathy towards yourself, you will feel that sympathy needed in others and will give it.
- Start to follow the correct life path that is showing in front of you because, as you start to own who you are, your beloved *Spirit* is already ahead of you and will have all sorts of ideas for you and will take you from there.

Be gentle with yourself.

A Lesson on Reflection

It is a very interesting word, *reflection,* and it is one of the quickest ways of stopping us from blaming, finding fault, or pulling other people to pieces.

A lot of society has been raised to play the blame game to make ourselves feel okay, and it doesn't matter which society you are in. You learn this game well, and as you grow up you become more judgemental. Some people enjoy gossiping and it doesn't matter if it's correct. It is like some newspapers – a lot of the time it doesn't matter if it's an accurate story or not. We read it and react.

On reflection, we know we do have a choice. And when thoughts and ideas are coming into our heads, we can choose to hold on to them or let them go and start again.

One of the most important things to remember is when we pick fault or play the blame game with another person, we are actually looking at ourselves. Yes, ourselves. Back to that interesting word, reflection.

We are seeing a picture of ourselves because we are recognising the behaviour coming towards us. You can only recognise a behaviour if you know it and if you have done it yourself. You are going to recognise it because it's a reflection. Remembering this is one of the quickest ways to stop us complaining about someone else's behaviour.

> **Gill:** I remember quite a few years ago now, Denny and I were having a big debate about this very subject. For the next few months, we were really good. We did not judge, we did not complain, we did not find fault in anyone else because every time we might have (because we are human, too), we stopped ourselves because we thought, "Oh no, I am not going to be judgemental about *that* person in whatever form because I recognise it in me." We laughed so much as we reminded each other to be good.
>
> Another time we were out having lunch somewhere, and it was taking a really long time to come. We were both desperately trying not to complain or moan at the fact 'they' were taking a very long time. So, we were really trying to restructure our words so that it was an observation rather than a moan! It really stops you.
>
> It is a good lesson, but it is also a good way of experimenting to see if we can change how we react, and of course by changing our behaviour, we are lightening the planet of negative chatter.

Look After Your Energies

It's a strength of character to look after oneself on all levels –
including energetically.

For example:

Imagine you are going to the supermarket, and you are walking
around the supermarket getting what you want. You pass quite
close to someone in the same aisle, and your energy field knocks
their energy field, and vice versa. Our energy field is a bit like
Velcro – it sticks and moves backwards and forwards. You, in that
one movement, will have done an exchange of energy without
realising it.

As you go around the shop, you continue to pick up energy
from other people and they will pick up your energy. If you pass
somebody in a temper, you wonder why you are feeling angry.
(This of course could be any emotion.) Often, at the end of your
shopping, you are absolutely exhausted, and you don't know why.

The main reason is that you have taken on so much stuff
energetically that belongs to all the other shoppers who have
been leaking energy all round their bodies when moving. None
of this energy is good for you. So, what do you do? Sieve yourself.

How to Sieve Yourself

- Imagine a garden sieve and how you sieve soil to get rid
  of the stones and clay. Same principle.
- When you come out of the shop before you actually
  pack or get in the car, you stand by the car.
- Think of a big wide garden sieve about 10 ft above you
  and the same around you. It's full of holes.
- Your intention is to clear out what's not your energy.

- In your mind, you gradually bring the sieve down over your body and watch it, collecting all the negative stuff that is not yours.
- You take this sieve all the way down your body – through your energy field – down to the ground.
- You ask Mother Earth to take and recycle the contents, which she is always very willing to do.
- Do it again. Now the holes are smaller, and you are collecting smaller negativity.
- Finally, once more. This time the holes are really small to collect the fine dust.
- It is the last of the energy that is not yours, does not belong to you, and is not friendly with you.
- As you send that final dust down to Mother Earth for recycling, thank Mother Earth for doing it.

A Note On Sieving:

The intention is to hold on to your own energy and take out other people's energy. When you give energy away, you are giving it away because it is not necessary for you and your body. Your thought process knows exactly what is relevant and what is not, and what it is doing when it sieves and removes only irrelevant material not of our making. Sometimes, it can be old and our own energy that is no longer relevant.

A Note To You

- You have always been perfect.
- You always will be, because *Spirit* chose you to come back down here into a human form to learn what *Spirit* cannot do when it simply is *Spirit*.
- *Spirit* hasn't got a body.
  It cannot feel emotion.
- *Spirit* just is love.

Love Is the Only Truth

Denny & Gill

CHAPTER 5

An Extraordinary Friendship

Gill: When I was sharing one of my drafts of this book with a friend who was very close to both of us, Rach asked me why I hadn't mentioned the special bond Den and I had. She said, "You were both so powerful together, in day-to-day living, and also in the workshops and meditation groups you ran together." Rach added, "Den used to say to me, 'Without darling Gill's help and support, I would not be able to help and support others. Gill always knows if there is pain."

It is true. I did know when Den was in pain and needed support. We tuned into each other. Words weren't needed a lot of the time. Den said, and Rach agreed, "We both have a deep spiritual bond, a connection like no other." Thanks, Rach for reminding me.

Denny Remembers Gill

Meeting Gill

In 1993, I saw a notice about the College of Healing and thought that it could be a really great training to help me grow. My daughter Clare, who was staying with me at the time because she'd been quite ill, signed up for the course with me. It was a long, long drive down, very enjoyable but a long drive to Malvern, where the College of Healing was. We arrived and parked, feeling totally lost. (I was wondering if I'd been a total nincompoop for signing up.) But we checked in, were shown to our rooms and then went exploring. We discovered a place that served tea, coffee, and alcohol. We went inside, and sitting there was a woman called Gill.

I looked at her, and she looked at me, and it was like part of me had come home. I had no idea who she was, but she was so familiar, it was scary. I think she was feeling the same because she had this strange look on her face, as if she was trying to work out who the hell I was. Then Clare, who had gone to get us coffees, came over and both Gill and Clare had the same response.

That was the start of our friendship twenty-eight years ago. We very quickly had the realisation that we knew each other very, very deeply. The friendship just gradually grew, and Gill would come up north and stay with me.

By working together, we discovered we had been twins in a past life and actually learned we had been twins quite a few times. We weren't twins in this life as we both had individual learnings to do, which, being twins, would have stopped us from doing.

So once the learning was complete, it appeared that we were allowed to come together again, and we have been together ever since. Gill is part of me. We seem to be walking side by side on our journey, just like twins might do. She is there for me. She looks after me. She puts up with an awful lot from me, and she is my greatest friend.

Over the years, we have experienced some amazing things, with *Spirit* setting up situations and learnings for the pair of us. A lot of the times, even though the learnings could be very deep, we always found a lot of laughter. From training in Eden Energy Medicine (EEM) – we very often would get things wrong and could be found giggling over a couch as we practiced on each other – to walking in the woods, getting terribly lost, and *Spirit* sending an elderly man walking his dog to guide us back to our correct path and our car, if I remember correctly!

Spirit Brings Me South

There I am, minding my own business up in the north of England. Very happy. Children all safe and at school. I am working hard and working well, and loving where I am, when all of a sudden, a dream started: "*You have to move south!*" I totally ignored it because *no way* was I going anywhere.

I had found my niche, everything was fine. It went on and on and on until in one of my stubborn angry moods I asked *Spirit*, "What on earth are you talking about?"

The answer was, "*You have to move south to enable your gifts to expand, to be able to do more than what you are doing in the north.*"

Having taken that on board bit by bit, I started to get a feel of where my body might like to be –would like to live – and I kept coming up with the Midlands. Geography was never my strong point, but I dowsed maps of England and landed up all the time around Birmingham. All that area, but not Birmingham itself, thank goodness.

Once I ascertained that it was the Midlands I was going to – this is where my guides wanted me to go – I rung my great friend Gill and invited myself down to spend the day with her dowsing the county of Worcestershire to see if this was the county.

Of course, it was Worcestershire, because that was the county that Gill lived in, and it was close-ish to where my ancestral family had raised their children. It's where my uncle, mother and aunt had been born. And so, I went down and stayed with Gill, and we had the most hilarious time, dowsing around Worcestershire, with more 'Nos' and more mental headaches than I think either of us had ever known.

It was about this point that we came towards the village of Evesham and the whole of the dowser sprung into life with an enormous, "Yes!" We drove across the river into Evesham, went to an estate office and asked if he could look at some houses around Evesham. And he kindly did. He was the most tolerant man – he deserved a medal for what he did – because I had been given a mental picture, and so had Gill, of exactly what I was looking for – grass all around, pointy roof, and a chimney.

We started looking at various properties but none of them looked like the description I'd been given by *Spirit*. Then one day we were given a property to look at and we arrived early and knew straight away it was a no.

As we were about to leave, the estate agent arrived, and when we told him it was definitely a no, he said, "There actually is a property close to here. The owner is a bit particular about who lives there, and it won't be advertised, but I think you might be a good candidate. Now, it's in Broadway and you may not have heard of the place, but it's in a private lane called Springfield Lane." To which both Gill and I nearly fell over. Of course, we knew it because that was where Gill lived!

We arranged to meet him the next day and as soon as I arrived, I knew it was the place. The description totally fit. The agent left us to look around and as soon as I got inside the door, my guides were jumping up and down, saying, *"What took you so long?"*

Yes, this was the house, but I still had to have an interview with the owner. Unfortunately, I had to rush back up north because my mother had been taken ill, and so I had my interview via the telephone. During the conversation, I was asked why I wanted to move down to Broadway, and I replied that it felt familiar because my mother had gone to Cheltenham Ladies College. Well, that sealed it! Because she had gone there as well! I passed my test and moved down to Broadway in Worcestershire.

Leo the Cat

Beloved cat Leo was grey and white. My children turned up with Leo, who they reckoned had been thrown out of a car as a little tiny kitten, and he was so frightened of life and so tiny. We took him in and he lived under the glass cabinet for probably the first week of being with us. He would not come out, but we put a stack of newspaper and a bowl of water, a bowl of food, and a litter tray which wasn't used.

He started to very gently emerge, and he just was so beautiful, but he became a people's cat, not a house cat. Cats usually relate to the surroundings and the people add on when they want to, but Leo didn't.

We called the cat Leo, after my beloved sister Bron, and he answered to his name. He grew and became a much happier cat, less frightened. He started to trust us and wherever we went, he came too. He'd walk up to Gill's house, to the pillar box to post some letters, and he'd arrive at Gill's house, who would always have something for Leo, and it was very lovely. Gill's house became like a second home. I ran a clinic up in Scotland once a month and Gill very sweetly took over, kept an eye on Leo, spending evenings with him, feeding and loving him. He seemed to be very happy with this arrangement. He would walk with Gill and have conversations with her.

We both felt gutted the day we had to take him to the vet and bid him farewell. After he passed away, I started hearing the footsteps of Leo on the stairs every night! Then, about three months later, an amazing thing happened. I was in my kitchen, and there was the most beautiful looking cat – young but absolutely beautiful – standing by the front door looking at me. I smiled and went towards him, and I was greeted with a lovely purr and stroking around the legs.

I then discovered there was no cat food, so I rang Gill and we both went down to the shops for cat food. I gave him his breakfast exactly as if it had been Leo, and a drink, while I had my cup of coffee to start my day. When he finished eating, I opened the front door, and he went out.

That night I went to bed, and there were no sounds on the stairs this time. But the next morning this beautiful cat that had visited us the day before, was sitting on my bed, just the way Leo used to sit. I realised it was Leo coming back to show me that his life was now fabulous. That he was OK and to stop feeling guilty about having to put him down. This was a most beautiful gift from his essence!

My Dearest Friend

What has kept me going all this time has been my dearest friend Gill. She has walked beside me, giving me so much help, care, and love – helping me to stay alive, which has meant I have been able to spread my teachings filled with knowledge, joy, and love to others, so that they too can spread this energy to others and get a reflection back in the world.

I laugh a lot and can weep from laughter. I find taking offence very hard. Because nine times out of ten, what they are saying is probably totally true.

When dear Gill and I were on our adventures, or just out for coffee, going places and getting lost beautifully – we would get lost in forests and woods, even in large hospitals – we end up laughing as we realise, "We've done it again!" No panic, just laughter.

Humour is very pronounced in Gill as well. It has us both loving life!

Denny & Gill Laughing

Gill Remembers Den

Yellow Noses and Daisies

When Den was still living in Cumbria, in Carlisle actually, I would stay with her. She lived near the river Eden and on this particular day, we went for a walk following the river. We came to a field that was full of cows and daisies. Suddenly, every cow's nose turned yellow, and every daisy turned yellow. Nothing else. I think we probably got the giggles and stayed watching this for quite a while and looking at it in total amazement.

We didn't want to leave but eventually we had to get back home. We asked *Spirit* what was going on? I mean, it is not every day you see yellow noses and daisies! But then, walking a path with Den was not only filled with fun and laughter, but unusual things too, and very *Spiritual* stuff.

Spirit's response was to get our attention, in a fun way, to say life is an illusion and anything is possible in life. So, there we go, anything is possible in life!

Third Time Is the Charm

Not long after Denny moved down to live five doors away from me in Broadway in the Cotswolds, I said to her, "Why don't we have a picnic? We put together a picnic and go off somewhere and I'll show you some of the sights to see in the area." Den thought that was a great idea. I said, "Where do you fancy going?"

"I don't know," Den replied. "What about Tewkesbury? What does that sound like? There is an abbey, a river, and part of the town is quite old and quaint. We are bound to find somewhere to have a picnic."

Our original plan was to go to the abbey first but decided that we would have lunch because it had taken us quite a while to get our act together, prepare ourselves and food to take, all that sort of thing. So off we went.

The first thing was to try and find somewhere to have a picnic. We eventually found somewhere. We managed to park up – so far so good – and we took our picnic with a picnic rug and discovered a massive field with no one in it. Plus, it was right by the river. We decided we wouldn't go too close to the river, but somewhere where we could watch any boats going by. We chose our spot, laid out our blanket, got all the food out, chatting away as you do.

We put the food out on the blanket and all of a sudden, we realised we were sitting on a rather large red ants nest! We moved. We packed up our food quickly, hoping we weren't taking any ants with us, and moved away to another area in the field.

We put the rug down, put all the food back out, and sat down again. We were closer to the river at this point and started chatting again and eating. Suddenly, a boat comes along the river and there is a group of people who are extremely rowdy. They are shouting, screaming adults, and really, really loud! To finish it off, they have decided to stop virtually in front of us. Really?

We sat there for a while thinking, "This isn't quite what we had in mind for our picnic." So, we have moved from the mountain of red ants, moved to where a boat stops with very loud people on it –they were so loud you couldn't even hear yourself think. Right. Shall we move again?

We packed everything up and sat somewhere else, far away from the noise because it was quite a large field. This time we were nowhere near the river, we were right at the back of the field.

We sat back down and got our food out. It was a lovely, sunny day and we weren't in a spiritual mood. We weren't really paying attention. We were there to have a time out and enjoy ourselves.

Now we are eating our food for the *third* time, and there is all blue skies and one cloud directly above us. Suddenly the cloud starts raining on us! Yes, just us!

Okay, life has got our attention. We knew we were being reminded to actually tune in and get a feel about any action we take, even where to visit. *Spirit* was trying to tell us, *"This is not right that you are here."* The energy wasn't right for us on that particular day.

We packed up. We didn't go and see the abbey. We went back home and sat on a picnic bench in Denny's garden and had our picnic. We actually felt we'd had our knuckles rapped, to be quite honest, although there was a lot of laughter. It was like, for heaven's sake, raining? The only cloud in the sky and it happens to be raining on us!

So, we were talking about it and actually tuned into Tewkesbury. Bearing in mind this was a very long time ago when Denny first came down to live in the Cotswolds, and when we tuned in, we realised that the energy of Tewkesbury was quite heavy. It is in the history books that there were lots of battles. When we tuned in, we could see that the river ran blood, so to speak. It was really heavy energy and basically *Spirit* didn't want us there. It took three attempts for us to pay attention.

It is worth saying that Tewkesbury has much better energy these days. I know a lot of work has been done on it energetically.

So, the moral is: *If you are given a sign, try and pay attention.* I mean, it took us a while to pay attention – we did have our off days, you know. We were not aware of things all the time. Sometimes we needed big signs to tell us to move, and then we did.

It did pull us up short to pay a bit more attention to places, people, and situations. *Spirit* does try to guide us, and can even get a bit tough with ant bites, sore ears, and wet clothes!

Trees and Angel Wings

Around twenty-four years ago, Den and I went on a little camping expedition for a few days. My son, who was quite young at the time, was going with the school on a five-day trip and so we decided that we'd go off camping and headed to our favourite campsite in Southwold, Suffolk.

We discovered that we'd actually be away during the summer solstice. The day of the summer solstice came, and *Spirit* said to both of us, *"There is some work we want you to do."* Right, well, Den was having none of it. "I am on holiday," she said. "I don't want to do any work."

As it was our last day, we visited a place called Dunwich Heath. As well as the heath there is a beautiful magical wooded area which is one of our favourite places to go. As we were walking, a beautifully blue dragonfly appeared in front of us. It was as though it was guiding us because every time we stopped, it stopped too, and once or twice, when we stopped, it appeared to fly right up to us and then back off along the track, as though saying *"Come on, this way."* It guided us down to a lower path into the wood. Then it disappeared.

During our walk amongst the trees, we came to a place where the energy changed, and our energies appeared to slow down and became still. We stopped. You could sense the fairies and the tree spirits. We both felt very strongly this was a place to stop and meditate for a while because, of course, *that* is not *working*. Who were we kidding?

Pictures of stones

We both went in search of a place to sit and connect to our respective trees. It was all so beautiful. I could feel the tree spirits and fairies around me and in my meditation realised I was connecting to the Merlin energy. I've always loved connecting to tree energy and I've channeled the energies many times before. Den was a short distance away meditating and connecting to the energies of the place.

Once we were ready, we carried on with our walking and were enjoying ourselves, when *Spirit* came in again and said, *"There is some work we'd like you both to do."* Den at this point was getting, (in her words), "Very bolshy." And she was having none of it, and she really didn't want to do it.

But I was hearing the words from *Spirit*, too. I was gently suggesting to Den that it might be a good idea to do what they were asking us to do. "No, no, no, no!" was Den's response!!! Early evening *Spirit* was still asking. and we sat with it, and I said, "Den, if we do this piece of work, they will probably leave us alone. It is obviously important because they are still asking."

By this time, it's semi-dark and we are back at the campsite with basic lighting. Den gave in to *Spirit's* request. We were told to go to the beach, which was very pebbly. *Spirit* said, "Go to the beach and collect ten or twelve stones each." The beach was just across the road from us, and off we went with a couple of bags, but of course by now it's totally dark and the only light is coming from the moon. Yes, our eyesight adjusted enough to see the beach and pebbles, but we couldn't see them in detail.

We brought them back and *Spirit* told us to make a circle of stones right next to our tent on the grass, which ended up being quite a big circle. Den was then asked to channel the energy of each stone and what it represented in the world, and more importantly, how each one was to help in the world. It really was quite extraordinary!

We knew this was important because of the way *Spirit* kept asking us to do this piece of work. Although we didn't totally understand how it would work, what we did know was that, as Den channeled for each stone, it activated an energy from the stone.

The next morning, we were packing up to head home, and the last thing we did was to collect the stones. We had been told that we could each keep three stones, and the rest we had to return to the beach. Of course, in the daylight we could see them properly. Each stone had a different design on it like a drawing. Some blue and others brown.

One had a very strong resemblance to a tree. We both chose that one and I chose one that looked like angel wings. Each design seemed to represent different things. Another stone had a loose stone within it which Den was told that she was to keep. When the loose stone fell out, she could then return it to the earth or the beach. We still have the stones today.

We both then had a bit of a moment. You would have thought that with everything that had just happened nothing would surprise us, but this did!!

When we lifted all the stones up from the circle, the grass underneath had all grown and was even greener. There was a circle about two inches higher than the rest of the grass!

When we took the stones back to the beach, we looked out to sea and right in front of us was a massive cloud in exactly the same shape as the tree on the stone! This cloud stayed in front of us most of the three-to-four-hour drive back home! We felt that maybe life was honouring the piece of work we had done.

Gill & Denny moving in to the bungalow in 2017

We talked a lot about that extraordinary evening and how, in the dark, we had been guided to the stones on the beach, each one a different vibration that activated different things around the planet. You think you are in control of life, planning and organising things you'd like to do. It's interesting how we both wanted to go camping for those five days whilst my son was away with school, to our favourite campsite, and it just happened in the right place and on the solstice when we did the piece of work for Spirit.

> "Life can be so fascinating when you work with Spirit!"

Our Bungalow

When Den and I were both living in the same lane, and Den got rheumatoid arthritis and started to really struggle, it soon became apparent – it was a no brainer really – that I should step up to support her, walk with her and care for her on whatever level was needed. My daughter said, "Why don't you share somewhere, Mum? You know, you both live in the same lane. You are both alone. Your kids have all grown up. Your husbands have passed away. Why don't you share? Be company. You can share the bills and I could keep an eye on Denny and make sure she doesn't misbehave!" And that is how we manifested our bungalow in Childswickham, Broadway, which has just been fantastic.

Country Roads with Grass Growing Down the Middle

One of the things Den and I used to do quite a lot was going on little adventures and it wasn't necessarily anywhere in particular, but we seemed to be finding ourselves on a lot of small country roads with grass growing down the middle. What was quite fun was discovering where these roads took us.

Usually there weren't any signs because it was such a little road it probably wasn't even on the map. A lot of the time we had no idea where we were going, but we were exploring. We really did have great fun and laughter in discovering where we would end up. We might be looking at a field of cows or there might be a little cottage at the end, or it might lead to a big road. Who knew?

We never gave up our little adventures enjoying our country roads with green grass growing down the middle. I was thinking about this, and for me that is part of the adventure of life, isn't it? It is exploring and not necessarily knowing where you are going, but just seeing where it takes you. It might take you somewhere and you have a jolly good laugh, and that will shift your vibration. We had lots of fun doing that, and it just seemed an appropriate thing to share. Go for it! Maybe you don't know where you are going – but enjoy the journey!

Going Home

*Denny got ill unexpectedly in June of 2021
and rapidly got worse in July.*

"It is the tools and the ability to very lovingly listen. Listen to your story, listen to their story. And bring together what is needed."

Gill and Denny Discover Something Extraordinary

Denny: I have been running very short of heart centre energy. So, with the help of one of our excellent colleagues, today we decided to go looking to see if we could find any reason.

Gill: Denny's inner core – her inner core energy – is really strong; really powerful and really strong. But her heart energy, it was like something was missing. We discovered that part of her heart energy was still in the orphanage, looking out for the two little girls that were in the orphanage when Denny was there.

Denny: I left them there and, on some level, I felt guilty all my life, which I thought had been dealt with. There was a strong connection between Lucy, Mary, and myself. We discovered the missing part of my heart was in our little bedroom in the orphanage. It was there, all the time, getting ready to rescue the other two. Although I consciously knew that they had both died years ago, I had still been trying to rescue them. This is what we did: We collected the essence of the two children and my heart became free.

Gill: You actually brought them into your heart today, didn't you?

Denny: Yes, yes.

Gill: It was beautiful.

Denny: Yes, they are now with me. It was like I was safe, and they weren't. But I had no idea that this is what I'd been doing, and why my heart was having such a tough time.

Gill: You might ask, "But why now?" We have been discussing this. We both feel it is because Den has been sharing quite a lot, talking about her early life recently. And because we are in the process of writing the book, it has allowed this energy to come up to the surface, to be looked at and worked with. This can happen in life – things come up to the surface to be looked at – if you can see them and don't get yourself in the way. Would you agree with that?

Denny: Yes, absolutely! It has been quite superb. I've got a lot more work to do yet, but it gives us a wonderful view of how our journey is going. How much better we are today. I have got to this next stage of my journey where I am able to smile and love these children without feeling I am having to rescue them. I am not worried about them anymore.

Gill: It is remarkable, isn't it? What you can do to help yourself and those that you have been involved with. You know, if you have the tools, you can work with that.

Denny: It is the tools and the ability to very lovingly listen. Listen to your story, listen to their story. And bring together what is needed.

Gill's Diary

July 18, 2021

As I write this, we are waiting for our dear Denny to pass over to the *Spirit* world. It has been quite a journey. It is fascinating being with her and watching her old physical body just as everything closes down. But her light – her light is so bright! Her core is so strong! You can almost feel those energies that have been working with her all her life are now getting ready to celebrate when she joins them again.

To have had the privilege of walking beside Denny, supporting her, guiding her, helping her with her needs as she suffered physically, but also having the laughs and the fun we have had, has been amazing! You know, it is extraordinary, the work she was doing. Sometimes, she did not even know consciously what she was doing, but her energies were splitting out and helping in all different directions while she was physically going about the normal stuff, as I would call it. But, you know, she was human. She *is* human. She has not passed yet, but what a special soul on this planet, what a special soul.

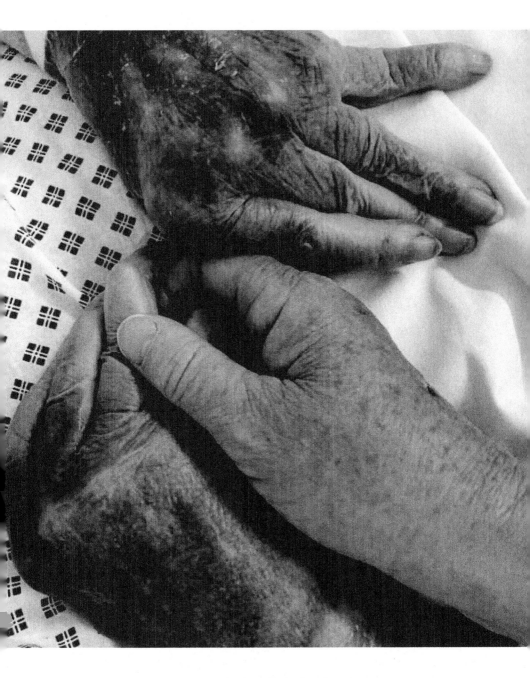

Denny's & Gill's Hands shortly before her transition

"I have done all this growth learning to the best of my ability, on behalf of Spirit. I will do so till my dying breath, and hope that somewhere along the line I have carried out some of Spirit's wishes in my muddled way."

A Farewell from Denny's Daughter Clare

July 19, 2021

Mum left the physical on 19th July 2021. My brother and I were by her side.

Lover of life
Lover of nature,
Lover of your family.
I will look for you in the sky
and everywhere in between.
Thank you for outrageous courage in the face of it all.

I wrote this poem for Mum about 20 years ago.
Actually, maybe I wrote it for all of us.

Love

Love beckoned me back to reclaim my heart,
To unravel a past that had taught me to close,
To unhook each moment less than light filled and shining.

And I came,
So that I might burn into a limitless sky
Unclad, unbound and breathing flames of truth
Shimmering slowly into remembrance
Each moment a melody
Each tear a death, a rebirth
And a yes to life.

Love beckoned me back to reclaim my heart,
And I have come to lay my dreams at her door.
Come to break my bonds,
That I might fall awake
Bathed in a bliss of tenderness,
Willing to trust her arms as my home
Willing to trust her heart
As I bless my own.

Gratitude

First and foremost, we would like to thank Dr. Clint G. Rogers and the Ancient Secrets Foundation for helping to make this book and Denny's dream possible. Without you, Dr. Clint, the world would have missed this beautiful treasure, full of wisdom, experiences, and helpful suggestions. Thank you from the bottom of our hearts.

We would also like to thank the many volunteers from around the world who have put in so much love and dedication; helping with transcriptions, editing, proofreading, creating the artwork, illustrations, and designs and in the making and shaping of this book and bringing it to life, a beautiful creation of Love.

Special thanks go to Francesca, Aparna, Abad, Bridget, Eve-Marie, Janet, Julia, Lisa, Rani, Rev. Michael, Sangeeta, Sharmini, Carol, Cornelia, Heidi, Maryam, Jahnna, Jason, Maggie, and Gen.

We would also like to thank everyone else who was involved in contributing to or funding this magnificent book, believing in it and feeling the LOVE in their minds, hearts and Spirits.

With so much Love and deepest Gratitude
Denny & Gill

Printed in Great Britain
by Amazon

22416001R00178